WARRANT FOR THE ARREST OF JOHN BUNYAN.

HEROES OF THE BAPTIST CHURCH

By

RONALD W. THOMSON

Author of

Modern Saints and Heroes
Missionary Prayers
Simple Stories about Saints
How Christianity Came to England
How Christianity Grew in England
How Christianity Spread in England

Foreword by

W. T. WHITLEY, M.A., LL.D.

LONDON
THE CAREY KINGSGATE PRESS LTD.,
6, SOUTHAMPTON ROW, W.C.1

Published, November 1937
Reprinted 1948

To Beryl
and her Mother

Made and Printed in Great Britain by
*The Carey Kingsgate Press, Ltd., London, W.C.*1

CONTENTS

CHAPTER   PAGE

FOREWORD 5

PREFACE 7

I. THE PIONEERS 10
    John Smyth, Thomas Helwys
    and John Murton

II. SOLDIERS AND PREACHERS . . 31
    Adjutant-General Allen, Benjamin Keach, and others

III. THE MEN WHO SUFFERED PERSECUTION 44
    Amongst whom was John Bunyan

IV. THE MEN WHO LED THE ADVANCE 56
    John Collett Ryland, Dan Taylor, and Robert Hall

V. THE MEN WHO LIT THE MISSIONARY TORCH 71
    William Carey, Joshua Marshman, and William Ward

VI. THOSE WHO BORE THE TORCH . 86
    William Knibb, Alfred Saker, Thomas Comber, George Grenfell, Holman Bentley, and Timothy Richard

3

PAGE

VII. GREAT ADMINISTRATORS . . 107
Roger Williams, Andrew
Fuller, A. H. Baynes, and
J. H. Shakespeare

VIII. "MR. GREATHEART" AND "MR.
VALIANT-FOR-TRUTH" . . . 137
Charles Haddon Spurgeon
and John Clifford

APPENDIX 155

BIBLIOGRAPHY 157

ILLUSTRATIONS

WARRANT FOR THE ARREST OF JOHN BUNYAN.
Frontispiece

Facing page

JOHN BUNYAN 46

ROBERT HALL 66

WILLIAM CAREY 73

TIMOTHY RICHARD 100

ANDREW FULLER 115

JOHN HOWARD SHAKESPEARE . . 121

JOHN CLIFFORD 137

CHARLES HADDON SPURGEON . . 138

FOREWORD

by W. T. WHITLEY, M.A., LL.D., F.R.Hist.S.

GOLD and jewels may be found by the patient explorer, even in unpromising river-beds; to fashion them, choose, and mount them attractively is a joy for quite another man.

Baptist annals, even in England, can yield to the digger some nuggets buried in the ordinary clay, but he is bound to tell how average and even under par is the plain man, the village church; only the eye of God unerringly discerns the jewels there. Meanwhile it is good when the cunning goldsmith selects one here and another there, disengages the true life, cuts the facets so as to catch the rays of divine light, and arranges the whole in a well-designed mounting.

Mr. Thomson has taken a fine handful of Baptist heroes, who illustrate many sides of our life. Evangelists, both at home and abroad, are easily first; statesmen receive unwonted honour; educators like Marshman are not overlooked. To many readers it may be a welcome surprise to find the various types of life illustrated. Yet there are even more than are here set forth; if these sketches gratify the appetite and whet it, they can easily be doubled with another series to set forth how variegated is the Baptist regalia.

PREFACE

THIS history of British Baptists is intended primarily for the young people of the churches, who have only a hazy notion of the growth of their denomination. That is inexcusable, and yet little has been written of set purpose for the young Baptists of the Fellowship and Christian Endeavour Societies. This volume is an attempt to remedy that omission.

The story of the growth of the Baptist Church in this land is one of absorbing interest. And, in the belief that it is more interesting still when seen through the great personalities concerned, I have largely presented the story by means of sketches of the lives of our great pioneers.

I hope that from this story, which I have tried to make short, easily readable and yet accurate, a fresh impression will be gained of the meaning, the vitality, and the responsibilities of our Baptist Church in this land.

I gratefully acknowledge the help I have received from the historians of the Baptist denomination, help so freely given; and also my great debt to my teacher—Principal H. Wheeler Robinson, M.A., D.D.—who first gave me an enthusiasm for these heroes and an appreciation of Baptist history.

July, 1948.

I am glad that this history has had such a good sale that the publishers wish to bring out a reprint; and I am especially pleased to know that it has sold widely as a prize-book for Bible Classes. This reprint differs from its predecessor only by a number of verbal alterations, the inclusion of present-day statistics, and the revision of the bibliography.

R. W. THOMSON.

"First and foremost, the glorious word and Evangel preached not in bondage and subjection, but freely and purely."

Declaration of aims of first Separatist Church, London, 1567.

"Yon is the man doth mitigate our cares,
He preacheth Christ, and doth God's word deliver
To all distrest, to comfort men for ever."

THOMAS HELWYS, *on a Puritan preacher in Newgate Prison with* HELWYS, 1612.

CHAPTER ONE

The Pioneers

TO consider the rise of the Baptist Church is to turn back to days when religious questions were a burning issue in the public life of the community. They were days when professions of faith were a common and open practice amongst men, and when differences in religious opinion were not politely disregarded. Religion was a force in the land in the seventeenth century, moulding the daily life of many thousands of the people. Religion was a force in the practical politics of the day, indeed, it was under the guise of religion that most of the political devilry and intrigue in Europe flourished. If it was in the name of religion that corruption and intrigue flourished, that was only so because religion was the governing impulse of the age, the deep and passionate concern of the multitude. It was a governing impulse of the day in a way this age cannot fully understand; and so, while it may seem to the present-day reader that it must have appeared a small matter some three hundred years ago that a section should have separated from the Established Church in England, it was no small matter in the history of the age. Every religious question was a burning issue in the public life of the community; and it was also of importance in its final outcome in this land, on the Continent of Europe, and in America.

Before the story of the rise of the Baptist Church can be begun, a glance must be taken at the general religious life of this country during the 16th century. It will be recalled that the Continental Reformation under Luther and Calvin had its repercussions in England, and under Henry VIII a reformation of the Church was carried out here. This was mainly to suit Henry's own purposes, and was a reformation more in

name than in fact. Henry asserted his head-
ship of the Church in place of the Pope,
making it clear that he was to be as essential
a factor in ecclesiastical as in civil
legislation. The Pope was declared by the
Convocation of Canterbury to have " no
greater jurisdiction conferred upon him by
God in the Kingdom of England than hath
any foreign bishop." The breach with
Rome was complete. Thomas Cromwell
became Henry's Vicar-General; in other
words, he was entrusted with the exercise
of the King's ecclesiastical powers. Cromwell's first act was to dissolve the
monasteries; but still, in spite of these
actions, the Church was to all intents and
purposes Roman Catholic in theology and
ritual. Indeed, in 1536 the " Ten Articles "
drawn up by Convocation showed that the
doctrines of the Church were still sub-
stantially the same as they had been before
the breach with Rome; the doctrines of
Transubstantiation (the change of the
bread and wine in the Sacrament into the
flesh and blood of Christ), the celibacy of
the clergy, the expediency of private

masses, and the confessional were all retained.

Mary undid much of the work of her father and her brother, but Elizabeth revived Henry VIII's ecclesiastical legislation. So that the only immediate effect of the reformation of the Church in England in the 16th century was the recognition of the King as the Supreme Head of the Church, the use of an English Prayer Book, and the free use of an English Bible. Naturally this did not satisfy the many whose spirit had been stirred by the Continental Reformation. They desired a further and more complete reformation of the English Church. So, during the reign of Elizabeth, a party arose which demanded a " purer " form of worship in the Church, which won its followers the nickname " Puritans." They conformed to the Church, for the most part, but they strove to alter some of the practices with which they disagreed. They disliked the use of vestments, they denied the right of bishops to " lord it over God's heritage," and many of them favoured a Presbyterian form of

Church government as being nearer to New Testament custom.

Some of the Puritan party went so far as to stay away from their parish church because they considered that separation from the Church would be their most effective form of protest. They were soon called " Separatists." They desired to set up at once a new Church more in accord with the order they found in the New Testament, and with Reformation theology.

A Separatist Church was formed in London under the leadership of Henry Barrowe, and one in Norwich under the leadership of Robert Browne. Browne was a well-educated man, in many ways a genius, and he brought the Separatist movement into public notice. He had the gift of a clear and vigorous style, and by his preaching, his writing and his intrepid spirit, he made the movement well-known. These societies which had separated from the Church of England were to be of more than passing importance. The ideals which dominated them, and which found expression in their demand for religious liberty, have profoundly influenced the subsequent lives of very many people in Britain, America and on the Continent of Europe. From such beginnings have come the Free Churches of England.

The story of the coming of the first Baptist church to England touches the religious life of the land at many points. Prelates and Puritans, Conformists and Nonconformists, all come into the picture. The lives of at least two very remarkable men are involved—John Smyth and Thomas Helwys. Within a few brief years these men separated from the Church of England, formed a new religious organisation, fled to Amsterdam to escape persecution, saw that the baptism known and administered in the Church of England was contrary to the New Testament, and established afresh a New Testament baptism. Later, one of them returned to England, bringing with him the seeds of the Baptist Church to plant in English soil.

* * * *

The parents of John Smyth sent him to Cambridge, where he became a student of the lower rank—that is to say, he received his keep and his instruction at a low fee, in return for certain services which he rendered. Cambridge was at that time in a turmoil over questions concerning the status of the ministry, and the right form of government for the Church. Francis Johnson, tutor to John Smyth, believed and preached publicly that the Presbyterian form of church government was the nearest to New Testament practice; for this he was imprisoned. After being released from prison, Johnson went to Holland as a minister to the English merchants there. Soon he took a further step, and coming back to London he joined himself to the Separatists, amongst whom he became an outstanding leader. It may be imagined that the young student John Smyth followed with interest the career of his tutor; no doubt he pondered very seriously the questions at issue. In 1593 Smyth graduated, and a year later was elected to a Fellowship, and took "orders." Some years later he was elected Preacher to the city of Lincoln, but his searching preaching soon incurred episcopal displeasure and the discontent of the City Fathers. It must have seemed to him at this time that the prospect of any national reform of the Church was hopeless, but he is seen next as pastor of a newly-formed church at Gainsborough, in a district where the Puritan element was very strong.

With the coming of James I to the throne all the hopes of men like Smyth were dashed. The various rules for the governing of the Church were consolidated, and the clergy were forced to give implicit obedience to them. The position of the Puritans grew impossible, and it became obvious that they must either accept the new rules or face imprisonment. About this time Smyth took the decisive step of forming his church at Gainsborough into a Separatist church, and people came to join him from many parts of the country. They were faced with many difficulties, but always they turned to the Bible as an explicit guide. Smyth renounced his orders, and became a simple member of the church, but his gifts marked him out for office as its minister. The covenant of this church is remarkable: the members were pledged " to walk in all His ways made known, or to be made known, unto them, according to their best endeavours, whatsoever it should cost them." They were ready to believe, as John Robinson (Puritan minister, and friend of John Smyth) said: " The Lord hath yet more light and truth to break forth out of His holy Word."

Smyth and his people were swiftly involved in difficulties. The machinery of the ecclesiastical courts was set in motion against them; some of the members were taken to prison; others were spied upon night and day; many had to leave the place. There seemed little possibility of their remaining peacefully at Gainsborough, and in the midsummer of 1608 they all migrated to Holland. In Amsterdam Smyth found his old tutor Johnson. Robinson, inspired by Smyth, also came to Holland, and settled with some of his own people at Leyden. The three churches of Johnson, Smyth and Robinson had friendly intercourse; but there were several differences in their practice, and soon the question emerged under discussion, "Who are the rightful members of the Church?" Smyth held that infants could not rightfully be baptised into it, but that the converted recruit was to be admitted by baptism. These two points were hotly debated, and a book in which Smyth expounded these and other points had a good circulation in Holland and in England.

Now Smyth was faced with a dilemma. He had rejected the orders of the Church of England, but he had not rejected its baptism. He had accepted believers' baptism as a necessary preliminary to admission into the church, and yet he had not renounced the baptism he had received as an infant. Accordingly he baptised himself, and then baptised all the other members of his church, saying that every person must make his own confession, and that by baptism. So the first English Baptist church came into being—but on foreign soil. Great interest was excited, many mocked at Smyth for his self-baptism, but he was at no loss to justify himself.

Smyth goes down in history as the first English Baptist, and an apostle of religious liberty.

*   *   *   *

Thomas Helwys, who was closely associated with John Smyth, was responsible for bringing the Baptist faith to England. The Helwys family was an influential one, it had been associated with the lower Trent valley for over two-and-a-half centuries. Edmund Helwys, the father of Thomas, had sold his lands in Lincoln and Northampton and had taken Broxtowe Hall, Nottinghamshire. On his death in 1590 his son Thomas took upon his shoulders the heavy burden of the family responsibilities. At the time of his father's death his education was unfinished, and so, although he was the sole executor of his father's will, Thomas continued his education for some time. He had been intended for the law, and was admitted to Gray's Inn three years after his father's death. Gray's Inn was then the most fashionable and the largest of the Inns of Court. Thomas returned to Broxtowe Hall after some twelve terms at Gray's Inn, and settled down to the life of a country gentleman. He seems to have prospered; when James made his Royal journey from Edinburgh to London he could have claimed knighthood, but did not do so, although his cousin was knighted at Theobalds. The sympathies of Thomas were very decidedly with the Puritan party; and Broxtowe Hall, through the kindly hospitality of Thomas and his wife Joan, soon became a second home for the Puritan ministers of the district: John Smyth was once nursed back to health there. The normal joy and brightness of the home was further enhanced when children came, but amid all his blessings Thomas Helwys took a very serious interest in the fortunes of the Puritan cause. When John Smyth, concluding that the whole system of the Church of England was beyond hope, started a new cause and gathered together his Separatist church at Gainsborough, Helwys became a member.

It was not long, as has been seen, before this church came into conflict with the authorities. Thomas Helwys could see that life in England was impossible, and he began to help in preparing for an exodus. He seems to have been instrumental in securing accommodation in Amsterdam, the city of religious liberty and home of many exiles. He even financed the removal of the church. Apparently he hoped that his wife and family would be allowed to remain in England unharmed, for he went without them. However, Joan was arrested and imprisoned, and Broxtowe Hall was seized by the Crown.

The story of the debates which ended in John Smyth's self-baptism and then the baptism of his followers has already been told. One of the followers whom he baptised was Helwys. Soon after these baptisms it was pointed out to the little church that a group in Holland called the Mennonites*

* Space has prevented mention of the Continental Anabaptist movement, which had culminated in the rise of the Mennonites in Holland (about 1536). These gave liberty to all to preach and to prophesy. The episcopal office was retained. The rite of feet-washing was observed with that of the Lord's Supper. Believers' baptism was practised by affusion (pouring). The term " Anabaptist " used of the Continental Baptists means " re-baptiser." The growth of the English Baptist Church is to be sharply distinguished from the growth of the Anabaptist movement on the Continent. There were big differences between the two.

held views almost identical with theirs : why had they not associated themselves with it? This fact was a surprise to them, and many readily agreed to join with this Dutch Church. But Helwys remained aloof, for he had found on examination that this church held very strong views about Succession, which to him savoured of Rome. This disagreement led to a division; Helwys, with some friends, broke away from Smyth. Interest now centres in Helwys, and Smyth leaves the picture, as far as the English Baptist Church is concerned.

As time passed Helwys became convinced that he and the others had been wrong in fleeing from persecution. He believed it to be his duty to return to England to bear witness to the truth; even to approach the King, and " to dare and challenge the King and State to their faces." Helwys, we must remember, belonged to a class that had the right of appeal to the King. He came to London in 1611, with some twelve followers, and settled in Spitalfields, which became the home of the first Baptist church on English soil. He directed from Spitalfields an appeal to the King to grant all his subjects full liberty of conscience: "The King is a mortall man and not God, therefore hath no power over yᵉ immortall soules of his subjects to make lawes and ordinances for them, and to set spirituall Lords over them."

It was not long before Thomas Helwys felt the royal displeasure, and Newgate Prison became his home. He died in Newgate, barely forty years of age. He seemed to have failed, but much came of that little church in Spitalfields, and of the appeal he issued so bluntly to all who thought as he did, that they should come "and lay down their lives in their own country for Christ and His truth."

This first Baptist church, which came to London the year before Shakespeare bought himself a house in Blackfriars, lived until nearly 1900. Four massive volumes of its minutes lie in the Guildhall Library, and portray the life of this one of the earliest of Free Churches in London. It did not meet in any building erected expressly for worship, but used an ordinary dwelling-house. In 1618 it was meeting at a place called Crosby House. Worship was only during the hours of daylight, since it was hardly safe to stir out after nightfall. Baptisms were for long carried out on the sequestered banks of the Thames at Lambeth or at Battersea. The Old Ford at Bow was a favourite place too. It was not until 1657 that the first building for baptisms was erected by London Baptists. In 1741 the original church of Helwys only numbered twenty-one male members; and yet it was in the same year that Thomas Guy, the Baptist Bible-printer, left £220,000 to found a hospital that still bears his name and still does devoted work.

On the death of Helwys the leadership of the cause passed to a fellow-prisoner—John Murton, a furrier, who led it for ten years.

*　　*　　*　　*

John Murton, on whom the mantle of Helwys fell, was born at Gainsborough in 1583. He was probably educated at the Gainsborough Grammar School, for he had a good education and a forceful, racy style of writing. He married Jane Hodgkin of Worksop. The two were well suited in age and outlook. Jane survived her husband, and returned, after his death, to Holland where she spent her last years in peace.

Murton took up the work of a furrier —a growing trade—in Amsterdam, and probably continued in the same business after returning to London with Helwys and the first little group of Baptists.

Murton spent most of his years in England in prison; and yet his literary activities were unhampered. In 1615 the English Baptists issued a book in which they answered such objections as were raised against them. The book bears no name, but it is almost certain that Murton wrote it. Later he drew up *A Most Humble Supplication* to the King and Parliament to redress their grievances, and lift the ban upon them. This supplication had no effect upon the King or upon Parliament, but its arguments were brought to the notice of Roger Williams in America. When he visited London he inquired as to the author, and was told how it had been written in Newgate, and how, having neither pen nor ink, Murton had been forced to write it in milk upon paper smuggled in to him. Other books came from Murton's pen, all supporting the Baptist cause.

The few Baptist churches in the country were closely knit together, but they sought contact with other Separatist churches, and they themselves continually sought to define their belief. To these ends Murton's literary activities were invaluable.

These churches clung very vigorously to the doctrine of baptism. It should be noted that baptism was then not by immersion, but by pouring. The mode was a secondary matter : what mattered was the principle of baptism as the basis of a regenerate church, an ethical act on the part of the baptised. Such a doctrine of baptism has not only emphasised faith as essential to the Church, but it has also, by its symbolism, constantly recalled men to the fundamentals of the Gospel.* It has thus taken the place of any formal creed in the Baptist Church.

* Romans vi. 3ff.

Other dominant ideas of the early Baptists were held in common with other Separatist churches. They may be roughly summarised : that faith concerned only a man and his God, it could not in any way be ordered by outside authority ("Christ only is the King and Lawgiver of the Church and Conscience," Smyth had said); that all members of the Church must be Christians; that the government of the Church should rest in the hands of its members. In the Bible they found the justification of this faith. They also had a living Christian experience which was their defence against ridicule and persecution alike.

Principal W. B. Selbie, M.A., D.D., in his book *Nonconformity, its Origin and Progress,* says of the church of Helwys and Murton that it "had the honour of being the first place in England where absolute liberty of religion and conscience was proclaimed. It was by the Baptists, in the first instance, that toleration was practised and that the full doctrine of religious freedom was maintained . . . . It was a long time before this spirit of tolerance and freedom was accepted . . . but the Baptists have the credit of being the first to state and recommend it."*

* p. 54f,

" Let none think that we are altogether ignorant what building and warfare we take in hand and that we have not sat down and in some measure thoroughly considered what the cost and danger may be."

THOMAS HELWYS, *Mistery of Iniquity*, 1612.

" To all the Saints and Churches of God, who walk according to the command of Jesus Christ in England, Wales, the *Army*, or elsewhere."

Faith and Practice of Thirty Congregations, 1651.

CHAPTER TWO
SOLDIERS AND PREACHERS

THE early days of the Baptist Church were days of persecution; again and again the churches had to face fierce opposition, and Archbishop Laud was one of the most prickly thorns in their side. But in spite of persecution they grew steadily. Murton and his followers spread the truth in two ways—by means of books and " apostles." These apostles were delegates who were sent wherever they were likely to obtain a hearing. With the purging of the Long Parliament, and the period of the Rump, came ecclesiastical liberty. The Little Parliament of 1653, called together by Oliver Cromwell, was nominated entirely by the Free Churches. Baptists and Congregationalists had every opportunity of showing what they could do.

The first period of progress amongst the early Baptists came during the existence of the New Model Army. The strength of Baptists in that Army, and the rise of Baptist churches wherever it went, and the fact that the most popular drill-books were written by Baptists is interesting. As early as 1644 William Packer, a Baptist, was a Lieutenant-Colonel and, when the Army was re-organised on a new model, it was under his guidance. Before long a very large proportion of Baptists were to be found in its ranks, and among its officers; this force was remarkable for a strong determination to win the Civil War, and in so doing to secure the complete liberty of the individual. Many a garrison had preaching by Baptist officers. At one time every commander, and the Commander-in-Chief in Scotland, was a Baptist.

Adjutant-General William Allen was an outstanding member of the group of Baptist officers. He was an earnest man, rugged and true-hearted; not easily governed, but with a steady head. He was one of the group of Army leaders who met for three days in prayer during the impasse to which Parliament and King had brought the nation. His name appears several times in Carlyle's *Letters and Speeches of Oliver Cromwell*. In time Allen lost faith in his leader. Cromwell and Allen had an interview, the result of which was that, when Allen went back to Devonshire, Cromwell ordered that he should be closely watched. Finally he was arrested, but he put up a vigorous defence, and was at last allowed to return to his post in Ireland. He wrote a booklet called *Word to the Army*, in which he reviewed the decline of the true cause, and said that the Army was guilty of Kingcraft. He had come to regard Oliver Cromwell as a worldly politician. Allen was a militant puritan, and his Puritanism was appalled at the thought that the motives of his old hero Cromwell had become tainted with worldly ambition. Allen was finally sent into exile for " endeavouring to debauch some of the soldiers from their obedience."

The names of some of the other commanders deserve mention, chiefly because, wherever they went with their troops, they founded Baptist churches. Dr. W. T. Whitley, in his *History of British Baptists,* says: "Colonels Rede and Deane traversed South Wales to stamp out a rising in Pembroke, and Baptist churches sprang up along their route. A Lancashire rising was quelled by Robert Lilburne, and within a month John Wigan had planted a Baptist church in Manchester. When the Scottish Army evaded Harrison, and came to grief at Preston, Brigadier-General Deane did fine service, while Rede helped capture the last infantry at Warrington; here again a Baptist church appears within three years . . . the cavalry besieged Pontefract and soon after its fall a Baptist church was found there."

The Continental Anabaptists objected to war on principle. Obviously the English Baptists disagreed with them. They had some difficulty in understanding the pacifist position, but this may be said of them: they did not keep their religion in a water-tight compartment. Let all honour be given to the men who were as great preachers as they were great soldiers, and who made it their business to leave Baptist churches behind them wherever they went.

*　　　*　　　*　　　*

Apart from the soldiers, however, during these years there was no outstanding leader for the Baptist churches. One of the reasons was that there were no paid ministers released from the daily struggle in the commercial world. The typical minister of the day was also a thatcher, a farmer, a blacksmith, a cheese-factor, a carpenter, a shipwright, a tailor, a butcher, a scrivener : ministers are known in each of these callings. The priesthood of all believers was thus illustrated in a very clear way, but it produced no outstanding leaders. The preponderance of the poor and the illiterate in the Baptist churches at this time also deprived those churches of the fellowship and service of men in higher places. Indeed, at this time we find but few Baptists prominent in trade or social life. Smith, Hills, Harris and Delaune were fairly prominent printers. One or two others owned coffee-houses in London. One kept by James Jones in Southwark received the attention of the authorities more than once, they feared that those who met in it did so for seditious purposes. William Kiffin is the best known of the merchants. Hanserd Knollys, originally a clergyman, then a schoolmaster, launched out into trade also. Richard Haines, of Horsham, tried to improve the lot of the agricultural labourer; he even patented a device for cleaning seed, but this was thought by his church to show a grasping spirit, and he was excommunicated. Peter Chamberlen became physician to the King. Of the career of Benjamin Keach, one of this very small group of prominent Baptists, rather more is known.

In his early days Keach was a tailor in Buckinghamshire. When about twenty-one years of age he was called to the ministry of the Baptist church at Winslow. He wrote a *Primer* for children in which he openly taught Baptist doctrine, so cutting across authority. For this he was arrested.

Chief Justice Hyde gave judgment at Aylesbury on October 9, 1664: " Benjamin Keach, you are here convicted of writing and publishing a seditious and scandalous book, for which the Court's judgment is this, and the Court doth award, that you shall go to gaol for a fortnight, without bail or mainprise; and the next Saturday to stand upon the pillory at Ailsbury for the space of two hours from eleven o'clock to one, with a paper upon your head with this inscription, ' For writing, printing and publishing a schismatical book, entitled *The Child's Instructor, or, A New and Easy Primmer.'* And the next Thursday to stand in the same manner, and for that same time, in the market of Winslow; and there your book shall be openly burnt before your face by the common hangman, in disgrace of you and your doctrine. And you shall forfeit to the King's majesty the sum of £20, and shall remain in gaol until you find securities for your good behaviour and appearance at the next assizes, there to renounce your doctrine and make such public submission as shall be enjoined you."

Keach was never brought to submission, or made to recant, but in accordance with his sentence he stood in the pillory in the market-place of Winslow on a certain Thursday in the autumn of 1644, while his book was publicly burned. Actually this incident was instrumental in bringing him to the notice of the London churches, and he was called to London a few months later. He rapidly came to the front in London, and was the leader in many new enterprises, including congregational hymn-singing. Apart from his *Primer* for children he wrote other books, amongst which was an allegorical *War with the Devil*. His books had a ready sale, and some assert that his allegory prepared the way for Bunyan's writings. He had included some hymns in his children's *Primer,* and later he published a collection of some three hundred hymns.

Baptists can be proud that they were thus the pioneers in this enrichment of public worship. Episcopalian, Presbyterian, and Independent clung vigorously to the Psalms, but Baptists were not so narrow. Moreover Keach was the first to introduce hymns into the regular worship of any English congregation. His book of three hundred hymns was called *Spiritual Melody.*

It is true that a minority of earnest members were scandalised at the thought of singing hymns " of man's composures." In a curious book printed in 1691, under the title *Breach Repaired in Good Worship,* Keach defended his innovation. He was careful to give Scriptural authority to his hymnal, which he did by drawing attention to such things as the hymn sung at the Last Supper.

The practice of hymn-singing grew. Ministers often summed up their sermon in verse—a new and a happy idea. And in the North manuscripts of such hymns and tunes circulated around the churches.

John Ash of Pershore and Caleb Evans of Bristol were the first to issue, in 1769, a collection of hymns by various authors. In 1787 Rippon gathered five hundred and eighty-eight hymns for use in the churches, and followed the collection with a book of two hundred tunes a few years later. He was not a poet himself, but he was a very judicious compiler, and his work obtained a large circulation. He laboured hard to improve many of the contemporary hymns, and his collection of tunes caught the public ear. The objection to singing modern tunes must have died down in his day, but it had been strong in some quarters. It is recorded that Rippon's predecessor, Dr. Gill, was approached by some members of the church who objected to the tunes they were required to sing. "What tunes," he asked, "would you like?" "David's tunes," they replied. "Well," he answered, "if you will get David's tunes we will try them."

The New Connexion was the first to have a hymnal owned by a denomination : that was in 1830. And the *New Selection of Hymns,* 1828, was the first in which the profits were devoted to the relief of the widows and orphans of ministers. Finally *Psalms and Hymns* was launched on its long voyage, so bringing the story down to modern times.

To return to the days of Keach : Baptists were pioneering to a remarkable extent. The work of a man like Thomas Collier is significant. His opponents called him "a base mechanical fellow, a husbandman," thus suggesting that he must have been a layman;

and as such he was typical of Baptist energy. For many years he planted churches from Guildford to the Bristol Channel. The Western Association—soon after its formation—appointed him General Superintendent of all the work in that area. His influence became enormous. He held debates with his opponents. He built many new churches, but not content with all this activity he began to use the press to supplement his work. In forty-six years he published nearly as many works. He issued a *Body of Divinity,* the first such work from a Baptist pen, but it had rather a poor sale. He was even drawn for a few years into the political arena.

Samuel Oates, a weaver, was another such evangelist. He preached in Sussex, Surrey, and Essex. In Essex he was arrested for murder because a woman whom he had baptised died within a fortnight. He defended baptism against George Fox, and published some small works.

Through such men as these the churches were slowly linked. That linking was invaluable, both in steadying the churches, in unifying their doctrines, and in aiding them in time of need. It was then that the name "Association" was suggested for such groups of co-operating churches.

It will be noted that few of these men had a University education; few occupied any notable social position: this was the general character of the denomination at the time. Indeed, they may not seem to have been of such stuff as heroes are made, but they proved themselves heroes during the time of persecution the Church passed through, as will be seen. Under the leadership they were able to give it, the Church weathered the storm that came upon it.

" Give me the liberty to know, to utter, and to argue freely according to conscience, above all liberties."

MILTON, *Areopagitica.*

" Now Faithful, play the man, speak for thy God,
Fear not the wicked's malice, nor their rod;
Speak boldly, man; the truth is on thy side;
Die for it, and to life in triumph ride."

BUNYAN.

CHAPTER THREE

The Men who Suffered Persecution

BAPTISTS desired nothing more than the rights of free men, they were not opposed to the paying of tithe for the support of the Established Church, but they did claim freedom to worship in their own way. The various groups of Baptists were all united in this, and in the cardinal points of their faith. Those points were broadly these : Christ commanded disciples to be baptised, then they must confess Him openly in that way; He wished them to commemorate His death, then the Communion service must be for those who had experienced His grace; He bade the disciples go and make more disciples, then the Church must be free to do so, and must be zealous in evangelising.

But the early Baptists were not allowed to do any of these things freely. The death of Oliver Cromwell, the dissolving of the Long Parliament and the Restoration of Charles II brought persecution once more. Clarendon, Lord Chancellor and adviser-in-chief to Charles, carried out a stern policy calculated to revive the Episcopal Church as it was before the Civil War; and once again Puritans had to suffer. The Act of Uniformity was so framed that no sincere Puritan could possibly remain as minister in an Established Church. The use of the Prayer Book, and the acceptance of its contents, was insisted upon. Nonconformists were therefore in a difficult, if not dangerous, position.

The result of this new outbreak of persecution was a rebellion. Certain Baptists took part in a plot to capture Charles. The plot miscarried, and they paid the penalty. After the death of Charles, James II pushed the persecution even further, with an attempt to bring Roman Catholicism to England. Monmouth and his followers rose, and many

Baptists were among the rank and file. Jeffreys hanged many of them, and the churches of Taunton, Lyme, Honiton, and Dalwood suffered severely. Elizabeth Gaunt, a Baptist, who had sheltered a fleeing rebel, was burned alive.

For many years Baptists could do little but just exist. James Jones, already referred to as a coffee-house owner in London, was also minister of one of the largest of the Baptist churches of the time. As such he came before an ecclesiastical court. He faced excommunication and imprisonment until such time as he should recant. However, he was wealthy enough to get sound legal advice, and found a loop-hole in the law. Unhappily his fellow Baptists were not so fortunate, and for many years prominent members of the Church were thrown in and out of prison. Sometimes their lives were threatened. The story of Bunyan is a case in point.

* * * *

One day a brazier, of humble parentage, was to be both seen and heard tramping down the streets of Bedford. He was to be

JOHN BUNYAN,
1628-1688.

heard, for no doubt he used the old tinkers' cry:

> Have you any worke for a tinker?
> Have you any old bellows to mend?

The brazier was tall; an attractive, well-built man, with reddish hair and sparkling eyes. He had a fresh face, the mouth and chin of a leader, and the eyes of a dreamer and a poet. He was a dreamer all his life; as a boy he had been tormented with visions of devils and had lived in a haunted world.

As a youth of seventeen Bunyan had joined the Army and had taken part in the Civil War. He seems to have been a wild youth, but marriage had sobered him, and he tells of attending church and of being moved by what he heard, " I went home when the sermon was ended, with a great burden on my spirit." And yet he still had some of his wild ways. One Sunday, while playing cat on Elstow Green, a voice sounded within him, reproving him: " Just as I was about to strike a second time, a Voice did suddenly dart from Heaven into my soul, which said, Wilt thou leave thy sins and go to Heaven, or have thy sins and go to Hell? At this I was put into an exceeding maze." From that day he tried to live a more godly life, but he was always racked with temptation and doubt. Then, while about his tinker's round in Bedford, he heard three or four poor old women sitting in the sun and talking about the things of God : " I heard, but I understood not, for they were far above, out of my reach." He could not get these people out of his mind, so he sought out their company and that of those like them.

It is almost impossible to enter into all the experiences Bunyan passed through; he had a restless mind, and its activity led him into great doubt and suffering. It was not, however, that he had doubts about God, the doubts were about himself : " I was greatly assaulted and perplexed, and was often, when I had been walking, ready to sink where I went, with faintness in my mind." At last he came out to certainty and something like peace of mind. John Gifford, the Puritan minister of Bedford, aided him. By his wise helpfulness Bunyan found the road that leads to the City of

God. Possibly Gifford is to be met as " Evangelist " in *Pilgrim's Progress* : " Then said Evangelist, Keep that light in your eye, and go up directly thereto, so shalt thou see the gate." And one day a small group might have been seen gathered by the river Ouse to pray for Bunyan as he was baptised by Gifford. He joined the Baptist community, but he was never a narrow sectarian; he was too catholic a spirit to be monopolised by any one denomination.

Bunyan soon felt the urge to preach, and was immensely popular as a preacher; his influence became unbounded. It was obvious that he would come under the notice of the authorities. He held strong views in regard to the Prayer Book and the Established Church. To the authorities, too, he must have seemed a wild, impertinent tinker, who claimed the right to preach the Gospel without ordination or sanction of any kind. It was thus inevitable that he should be arrested. He was kept in prison for twelve years, with one short break. In prison he grieved very deeply for his wife

4

and family; it seemed to him that he had brought nothing but ruin and pain upon them : but he would not submit. He busied himself making laces, and in dreaming and writing. He wrote in all some sixty books.

When Bunyan regained his liberty he became minister of the church at Bedford, but after a few years he was again arrested. During this six months' imprisonment he wrote the greatest of his books—*Pilgrim's Progress*. In the first year of its publication two editions were sold out, and it soon made the fortune of the publisher, but not of Bunyan. The fact that this immortal book has been translated into more languages than any other book in the world, save the Bible, is evidence of the way it has gripped the imagination of the world; and yet some of his friends urged him not to print it, saying it was but a fairy tale and therefore could only be of the evil one. However, on December 22, 1677, Mr. Nath. Ponder entered it at Stationers' Hall : " Entered there for his copy by virtue of a licence under the hand of / Mr. Turner, and which is subscribed / by Mr. Warden Kerr, one book a / copy Entituled, *The Pilgrim's Progress from this world to that / which is to come*. Delivered under ye similitude of a Dreame wherin is discovered his / setting out his dangerous journey / and safe arrival at the Desired / Country, by John Bunyan." The lumbering hand-printing press had to work at high speed after that; the row of small volumes, priced at one shilling and sixpence each, went as fast as the printer could produce them.

Many have asked what is the secret of the hold *Pilgrim's Progress* has had upon generation after generation. The secret is not hard to find, for this book has all the ingredients which attract readers. Here is a tale of wayfaring men; of adventure and romance; giants and highwaymen; castles and haunted valleys. And then, down the King's Highway move living men; whatever their strange names they are real people. Underneath the whole story is a meaning; it is the story of human experience, clear to all simple and imaginative minds.

Then it is a story with humour in it; and the chief character—Christian—is not of an irritatingly faultless kind; he blunders like the rest of us; indeed, he is one of us. Finally this book has a swift, decisive touch; many writers have the ability to describe a thing; Bunyan made his reader see the actual thing.

The last days of Bunyan's life were very happy, for he was loved and honoured by all. He died in 1688, sixty years of age, in the home of a friend in London. The house was named " The Signe of the Starre." It was fitting that he who so faithfully followed the star, singing joyfully of his experience, turning the Gospel into a song and a romance, should die under " the Signe of the Starre." " All the trumpets sounded for him on the other side."

Bunyan was a dreamer; he had visions, and he was a poet. He read men as clearly as most people read a book. He was always serious, but he refused to be solemn; he was no gloomy fanatic. His knowledge of the Bible was profound; he literally spoke its language, and thought its thoughts.

He saw the life of faith as an adventure, and for him this adventure was not all trouble and pain and disaster : it included happy joys, and quiet resting-places, and lovely, shining hopes. Bunyan, it is true, was abnormally introspective, but of his genius there can be no doubt. In his own personal life he walked very closely and humbly where God called; and through all stumbling and failure he marched home. Bunyan was no saint; like the rest of mankind, like his own "Christian," he was a faulty, blundering, struggling mortal; but he was also Mr. Great-heart, and Mr. Valiant-for-Truth.

In Westminster Abbey there is a window in his memory. Dr. John Clifford, entrusting it to the care of the Dean and Chapter in 1912, said : " This window is not only a valuable addition to the art which enriches and distinguishes this temple of fame : it also commemorates one of the most powerful books ever written by one of the greatest saints, but chiefly this work is a memorial of one of the saints who, through ' grace abounding to the chief of sinners' still continues his ministry to men, and will from this spot witness to the fundamental facts of Christian experience, and to the growing catholicity of Christian men all over the world."

*   *   *   *

Before the death of Bunyan, King James issued a Declaration of Indulgence, suspending all laws against Dissenters. From that day Baptist preachers, like Bunyan, no longer had cause to slip into meeting-rooms by back doors. The persecution was ended; the days of prison, pillory, and fine were over. Through those difficult days Baptists had maintained their ideals, they had stood firm; and they had been loyal to King and Country so far as conscience permitted. They had risked life, liberty, and wealth in their love of truth and their zeal for the spreading of the Gospel.

" Such societies have been formed . . . for village and itinerant preaching, as were never before heard of among the Baptists."

JOHN RIPPON, 1798.

" I'll go and try."
Last words of JOHN COLLETT RYLAND.

CHAPTER FOUR
THE MEN WHO LED THE ADVANCE

A CHARGE sometimes brought against Nonconformity is that it is merely negative. Such a charge comes from an inadequate knowledge of its history. Familiarity merely with the first few years of Free Church history might lead to such an assumption. Baptists and others for long seemed to do little but oppose the official religion of the State; they fought with sword and pen and voice against all tyranny and persecution.

Some slight attempt must now be made to assess the work these Puritans did. They have been more easily caricatured than understood by historians.

The Puritans represented a leaven in

England. Their protest against moral, political, and religious corruption and formalism was altogether timely.

They were not the illiterate men they have too often been pictured. Their leaders were nearly all members of one or other of the universities. The name " Nonconformist " was first given, for instance, to the *clergy* who would not conform to the law, especially the law regulating the use of the Prayer Book. A number of the laymen, too, were, as has been seen in respect of Helwys, men of sound training and good family. They had a great zeal for education, and were far from being merely disagreeable fanatics. They took their religion seriously, and believed in the kingly rule of God over their lives. They were both mystics and men of action. It is true that they had the intolerant spirit of their age, and many developed a self-righteous spirit; but it must be remembered that they were fighting all the time, and many had suffered bitterly under persecution.

It is often said that the Puritans failed.

It is more true to say that they were in advance of their age and, in the reaction that followed the Restoration, much of their work was destroyed. But their spirit lived on in English religious and social life. They were the champions of the rights of the people, of religious and civil liberties.

Carlyle says of these men that they represented " the last of all our heroisms. No nobler heroism ever transacted itself on this earth."

Dr. John Stoughton, in his *History of Religion in England from the opening of the Long Parliament to 1850,* says of these men that they, " not without some mistakes, but with a wisdom and heroism which it would be idle to question and unthankful to forget, secured for us those national privileges which distinguish England from the rest of Europe." (Vol. I., p. 51.)

Let it be clear, then, that Baptists, among this body of Puritans, stood for a positive faith; a faith as definite and as urgent as any for which any Church has ever stood. The contribution Baptists had to give the world was not so much the insistence upon a rite, as the insistence upon the freedom of the Church and the missionary purpose of the Church. Evangelism and liberty are the foundation stones of the Baptist Church.

Now the time for protest, pure and simple, was over. The days of active persecution were past : now the Church was free to advance. Would it have the power to do so?

It must be remarked, in passing, that the 17th century was one of the most momentous in the history of human thought; it was the century of genius. For instance : Bacon died two years before Bunyan was born. In the year of Bunyan's birth, William Harvey published his discovery of the circulation of the blood. When *Grace Abounding* was published, the Royal Society had just been formed. Robert Boyle was experimenting throughout the whole of Bunyan's literary life. Newton published his great work *Principia* the year before Bunyan's death. It is not suggested that Baptists in general were conscious of the great currents

of the 17th and early 18th centuries. For
the most part they would be in complete
isolation from them, but the time was one
of great changes, externally, and in the
mood and thought of the age. Would
Baptists be able to seize their opportunity?
Would they go out into the new towns that
were springing up?

*   *   *   *

For long it seemed as if Baptists would
not be able to seize their opportunity; there
was a great lack of vision and enterprise;
and then gradually the cause was re-
juvenated. This rejuvenation was largely
due to certain men, of whom John Collett
Ryland was one.

Ryland was an impetuous, headstrong
youth. While in his teens his father gave
him a horse. John at once bought a pair of
spurs, and the faster the horse galloped
the more he spurred him. It ended by the
horse throwing him against a bank and
leaving him there, bruised and bleeding.
This was the impetuous youth who was
captured by Pastor Benjamin Beddome.

During his pastorate at Bourton-on-the Water, Beddome sent six young men into the ministry, and Ryland was one. Through Beddome's influence he reached the Baptist Academy at Bristol. At Bristol the eager youth was rather discouraged by the discipline, and passed many unfavourable judgments upon his tutor. Later in life he wrote of the same tutor in characteristically sweeping terms— " Foskett should have spared no pains to educate our souls in grandeur, and to have enriched and impregnated them with great and generous ideas of God in His whole natural and moral character, relations and actions, to us and the universe. This was thy business, thy duty, thy honour, O Foskett! And this thou didst totally neglect." But the promise of Ryland's gifts and ardour was amply fulfilled. At the age of twenty-three he was invited to Warwick, and after he had been on probation for four years he was ordained in 1750. Such was characteristic of the deliberate action of the time. Ryland, with his ardent enthusiasms, was appalled at the dullness and depression existing in the churches. He tried to get into touch with his fellow ministers, but failed with some forty. He made a survey of the churches, and it was far from encouraging. He found in London, for instance, twelve ministers. Seven of the twelve were prolific authors; three of them were found worthy of honorary university degrees; and yet between them they numbered only 610 church members. Yet this was at a time when the Evangelical Revival was gaining strength every year. It had obviously not reached the Baptist churches, they were less touched by its influence than were far away Colonies in America; but a new era was soon to open. Ryland's enquiries stirred the Western Association and others. He moved to Northampton, and a new Association was shortly formed there. This Association began to send out circular letters dealing with a definite topic, in order to teach and encourage and link the churches. These readable pamphlets did their work well. Ryland understood the power of the Press and used it freely. He saw also that the general level of education must be raised, and so he began to devote himself to education, opening both boys' and girls' schools, and writing many of the school-books himself.

Ryland had his limitations, and in time he lost the impetuosity and enthusiasm of his youth. In consequence, when another young insurgent came to the fore—William Carey—Ryland thundered against him on the score of his youth and his enthusiasm: "Sit down young man, you're an enthusiast." The ageing man was losing his grip; and yet his last words were like the man: "I'll go and try."

*   *   *   *

If the Midlands, through Ryland and others, began to be strangely "warmed," the North was not far behind. Indeed, Baptist churches as a whole were now beginning to be influenced by the growing change in religious temper caused by the Evangelical Revival. In the North, Dan Taylor, a stone-mason, was converted by Wesley. He became convinced of the truth of believers' baptism, but the ministers in his neighbourhood were unwilling to baptise him owing to his views on the Atonement. All they would do was to send him and his friends to the Baptists of Boston, who shared Taylor's views. Taylor was eventually baptised in 1763. He joined the Lincolnshire Association and was soon ordained to the charge of Wadsworth. He undertook a begging tour through the Midlands in order to pay for a new meeting-house, and down in Leicester he came into touch with kindred spirits. These Baptists inspired him to build his meeting-house with his own hands.

Not only did the Leicester men inspire Taylor, he inspired them with his own zeal and driving force. Together they looked up particulars of old organisations and planned a wide re-organisation of Baptist churches. Churches and mission stations multiplied rapidly, and with great enthusiasm an Assembly of Free Grace Christians (or New Connexion) Baptists was formed. Many churches rallied to this organisation. The old Evangelical flag had come into courageous and daring hands, and the command was given to advance. Dan Taylor was an inspiring leader and administrator. In travels, and in much else, he was the Baptist Wesley.

Taylor had learned the need of education. He accordingly founded a school. But that did not content him and he began to plan greater things. He decided to open an Academy for ministerial training, and he was soon sending out young men into the ministry.

With Samuel Deacon, Taylor compiled a book of two hundred and ninety-three hymns for the use of his churches. The book was quickly in wide use. In every possible way he directed the enthusiasm of the churches to practical ends. He founded and edited a denominational journal—*The General Baptist Magazine*.

*   *   *   *

There were others besides Ryland and Taylor who desired a revival in the Baptist churches. Caleb Evans and many others helped to rejuvenate dying churches and to revive old Associations.

5

To the village of Arnesby there came in 1768 a man of sturdy northern stock—Robert Hall. He and his 14th child, also named Robert, were leaders in the forward movement. Robert Hall, jun., had received his education at Ryland's school at Northampton. He told in later life how he was taken there by his father. It was the time of the American War of Independence. Ryland was against his own Government. Very dogmatically he burst out to the elder Hall with the declaration that if he were General Washington he would have his officers bled into a punch bowl; then they should dip their swords in the bowl and swear never to sheathe them while an English soldier remained alive in America. The small boy, who tremblingly heard that, was to be a great preacher. He was a boy who at nine had read and re-read Jonathan Edwards on the *Affections* and the *Will,* together with Butler's *Analogy.* It was with difficulty that his passionate thirst for knowledge could be quenched.

After his schooling at Northampton in

ROBERT HALL,
1764-1831.

Ryland's school, Robert Hall went to the Bristol Academy, and then on to King's College, Aberdeen. He held four pastorates, and was a pillar of the Church, a great figure of the day.

Hall played a large part in reviving the churches and in bringing a wonderful change over the denomination. As a preacher he was recognised as a genius; his fame ran through the land. One sermon of his was published and went into sixteen editions. He had a great command of words; in an *Apology for the Freedom of the Press and for General Liberty,* he denounced Pitt as " a veteran in frauds while in the bloom of youth."

Robert Hall had undaunted courage and resolution, and yet all his life he suffered acute pain. In the increasing pain which visited him towards the end of his life, he dwelt often on the sufferings of Christ. His mysterious malady—not diagnosed until a post-mortem was held—tortured him incessantly, but he rose above that torture. Like St. Paul he found Christ's grace sufficient, and His strength made perfect in weakness. His was the true triumph of spirit over bodily infirmity.

* * * *

All through these and the following years the face of England was changing with the coming of machinery driven by water-power. Towns began to grow at an extraordinary rate. To these new towns Baptists came, and they appealed with success to the workers of lace and stockings in the Midlands, of woollens and cottons in the Pennines. Evangelists went into the mining areas. From Rawdon the cause stretched out to Gildersome, Bradford, Shipley, Farsley, Bramley, Leeds, and Halifax. The steam-engine (a new power harnessed to the new machinery) brought a further rapid increase in the population of many towns, and in all these towns new churches were formed. The Baptist Church was advancing. Many leaders led this advance; many more leaders grew up in these new churches. In time these churches became the training-ground and the university of the working man. Here he studied the Bible, educated himself, learned to organise and administer; and from these churches he began to look out upon the world with new eyes. The time of rejuvenation had come to the Baptist churches.

" O let Thy blessed Gospel shine
That the blind heathen may be Thine."

From Hymn No 127, written by KEACH.

" Whether the command given to the apostles
to teach all nations was not obligatory on all succeed-
ing ministers to the end of the world, seeing that the
accompanying promise was of equal extent? "

The question raised by WILLIAM CAREY
at a meeting of ministers in 1786.

CHAPTER FIVE

THE MEN WHO LIT THE MISSIONARY TORCH

THROUGH the years, since their birth, the Nonconformist churches had been claiming from kings, statesmen, and ecclesiastics the freedom to think and preach according to their own conscience. Then had followed a time of consolidation, and then of revival and extension; there was much to be done, many tasks to absorb their strength. All this explains the self-centredness of the churches. But that explanation does not excuse them. " In the very centuries when our fathers were insisting upon larger national and civic and religious liberties for themselves, they stripped hundreds and thousands of Africans of every vestige of freedom. They martyred the Dark Continent. Instead of carrying thither the torch of the Gospel, they lit therein the fires of hell."*

* S. Pearce Carey, M.A., *William Carey*, p. 7.

At last there came into this darkness of selfishness and of indifference to missionary enterprise, certain men with a passionate zeal for Christ, and a burning desire to win the whole world for Him. A few individual Christians began to care for heathendom, and these men lit in the hearts of others the same passion. Three names stand out in Baptist history—Carey, Marshman and Ward. Carey was the greatest of the three, but Ward and Marshman were indispensable to him. Dr. John Thomas was also with them in the early days. These men set the example which missionaries have followed since, in every land.

When in 1801 Carey, Marshman and Ward laid the first Bengali New Testament on the Communion Table—the result of seven-and-a-half years of labour—they were consecrating Christian scholarship to its great task of giving the citizen of every land the Bible in his own tongue. When Carey in the same year went to occupy the Chairs of Bengali and Sanskrit at the Government College in Calcutta he opened the door to all the educational work which

WILLIAM CAREY,
1761-1834.

missionary societies have carried on so brilliantly since. And when Krishna Pal had his shoulder treated by the skilled hands of John Thomas, and the way was opened for the Saviour to enter his heart, John Thomas was setting the example for those medical men who should later lay their gifts at the feet of the Master for His use.

These pioneers of modern missionary enterprise deserve attention, and as each of them falls into his appointed place by the side of William Carey, attention must first be paid to this man whose work has meant more to India than that of any Viceroy England has sent out.

*　　*　　*　　*

William Carey, as a boy, seemed to have no chances. He was born in one of the humblest cottages in the village of Paulers Pury, Northamptonshire. His father was a small handloom weaver. William had little schooling, at twelve he was out earning his own living. He tried gardening, for he was passionately fond of gardens and gardening; but his health was not strong enough. His father therefore bound him to a shoe-maker. In spite of his health, Carey was always adventurous. One day, as a boy, he longed to possess a certain nest in a tree top. He tried to climb the tree, but fell, hurting himself badly. For some weeks he had to remain in bed, but on the first occasion that his mother left him he went out and climbed it again; she found him on her return, sitting by the fire nursing the nest. The only thing he would say to her was this: " If I begin a thing I must go through with it."

Carey's great hero was Columbus, and then later Captain Cook. He was thrilled by reading Captain Cook's adventures. A fellow-apprentice won him for Christ, and persuaded him to join the local Baptist church. That turned Carey's love of adventure and exploration into a new channel: why should not the Christian message be taken to Cook's South Sea Islands? That became his dream. There appeared a vision to him, a Tahitian saying, " Carest thou not that we perish? Come over; come over and help us."

Carey began to preach, and was soon ordained as the minister of the little church at Moulton, at a salary of four shillings a week. He made maps unceasingly, he read his Bible with deep interest, he studied Latin, Hebrew, Greek, French, and a little Dutch. He made a globe of pieces of leather, and on it he claimed in vision the kingdoms of the world for his Christ. He went to Leicester as minister, and his sermons there were constantly on the theme of missionary enterprise. He had hard work in persuading others to accept his arguments; his fellow-ministers were particularly hard to win. Old John Collett Ryland grew angry with him for meddling in God's affairs : " When God wills to convert the heathen world, He'll do it, and without your help or mine." But no one could silence William Carey. He wrote *An Enquiry into the Obligations of Christians to use Means for the Conversion of the Heathen*—a strong case for missionary work. But this, and his immortal sermon in Nottingham to his fellow-Baptists on Isaiah liv., verses 2 and

3—with the two heads, " Expect great things from God " and " Attempt great things for God "—did not move them to action. They answered that they had neither sufficient strength nor funds to do this work. But Carey had a great friend, Andrew Fuller, whose spirit matched his. Fuller called some fourteen ministers together at Kettering; they had not much influence, many of them were unknown outside their small village circle; but they found sufficient courage to form the Baptist Missionary Society in 1792. Those few men promised subscriptions totalling £13 2s. 6d., a ridiculously small capital with which to launch a missionary society —none of them earned more than 13s. a week—but God was behind the project. They were attempting great things for Him, they were to prove that great things were possible from Him. Within a few months their thirteen pounds were multiplied by thirteen; and the small society, formed that day, was the beginning of many great missionary societies. Within a century the twelve-and-a-half guineas had become five million pounds a year, and the one man ready to go had become a band of twenty thousand men and women sent out by over five hundred societies and organisations.

'Now at the time all this happened a John Thomas, a Baptist, and a ship's surgeon, came back to England after many years in Bengal. John Thomas was impulsive and erratic, but in Bengal he had been moved by the plight of the people and had done all he could to help them. He had the soul of an apostle. For seven years he had been their teacher and their doctor. He learned of what had happened at Kettering, and he begged that Carey would go back to Bengal with him. Carey felt that it was a call of God, and, although his heart had been set on going to the South Seas, he joined Thomas.

Carey and his family were faced with destitution when they arrived in India, but a way was opened and he became a farmer and planter. Hope sprang up in his heart also when he and Thomas were given the managerships of two indigo manufactories. This meant a fixed salary. Each was brought into contact with the peasants, and had more opportunities for learning the language and for spreading the Gospel. The two men made the utmost of these helpful conditions. Carey ceaselessly tramped round the district, preaching the Gospel.

Carey found that India was in a terrible plight : babies were sacrificed in the Ganges, men swinging from the flesh hooks drew great crowds to the festivals, India's widows were taught that it was their glory to burn with the body of their dead husband, and in Bengal alone some six hundred were burnt every year. He found the ignorance, and the evil, the waste of womanhood, the cruelty of the priests, and the inhumanity of the caste system truly terrible. To make it worse, the merchants and the soldiers sent from Britain were living godless, evil and immoral lives. If these last-mentioned people had known of the thoughts in the head of that little man, so frail to all appearance; if they had suspected the high-explosive in his frame, they would have hustled him out of the land.

Indeed, in 1800, when other missionaries came to help Carey, they were not permitted to land, and so the whole party, with Carey, moved to Danish territory at Serampore, where they knew they would be allowed to go about their work in freedom. Two men of the finest type now became partners with Carey—Marshman, a schoolmaster, and Ward, a printer. Carey had no converts to introduce to them, in spite of all his toils; up to this point there was not one convert to show.

Marshman and Ward had brought funds with them. This enabled Carey to concentrate upon the printing of his Bengali Testament. Ward was a printer and he at once set up the printing press which was to accomplish the greatest achievement in the history of missionary literature. Marshman began to found schools.

About this time Lord Wellesley, Governor-General of India, realising that his civil servants needed a thorough training in the languages and customs of the people they must rule, decided to establish a college at Calcutta. This college was opened in

1801 and, although the Provost and Vice-Provost were Anglican clergymen, Carey was called to become tutor in Bengali and Sanskrit. So a despised Baptist missionary, self-appointed exile in Danish territory, was called to responsible service at the heart of India. Under his influence were to come the future rulers of India.

Apart from the influence this post gave Carey it also brought him wealth, but every penny he made went into the mission.

Slowly a stream of converts began to come in. Krishna Pal was the first. Krishna Pal, a carpenter of Serampore, fell and dislocated his shoulder. After setting his shoulder the missionaries told him about Jesus. Through many days they talked and talked to him of this Saviour, until at last they won him and his house. That one Indian Christian home became the base of a swift advance.

Marshman and Ward were invaluable to Carey. Both were devout, and yet intellectual, free from petty jealousies, devoted to India, abounding in energy, dedicated passionately to the service of

Christ. From first to last they gave all their large earnings to the mission. Carey must have contributed some £40,000 from his professorships, Marshman probably a like sum, and Ward several thousands from the profits of his printing press. In scholarship they rivalled each other; they were scholars of great thoroughness and zeal, and all their talents were consecrated to one purpose— the extension of the Kingdom.

Carey translated the Bible into six of India's chief languages, the New Testament into twenty-three, and parts into many other languages. Altogether he translated the whole, or parts of the Bible, into thirty-four of India's tongues. He wrote grammars and dictionaries. He translated India's wonderful epic—the *Ramayana*—into English. He established a native press and magazines, and also a newspaper for Europeans. When he died, Marshman said "He hasn't left us any original translation work to do." The greatest thing he did was to translate the Bible into Sanskrit, the language of India's scholars.

These tasks were not carried through

6

without troubles and difficulties. At home, and in India, scorn was poured on Carey. Nothing, however, could daunt those three heroes, not even the great fire of 1812, when their printing works were burnt to the ground, and priceless manuscripts and types were ruined. The foes of missionary enterprise were full of joy, but those three men were not broken. Within twelve months they had made good the damage, indeed, in some things—for instance, their printing type—they had taken the opportunity to improve upon the past.

Next Carey built, with his colleagues, a great College at Serampore, to which the King of Denmark gave a full charter, with power to confer degrees. It is held to be the most beautiful building of its kind in India. Round it Carey built an amazing five acre garden, the finest in the East. The poorest of India's sons are admitted to the College, and there the best wisdom of the East, the science and literature of the West, and the glory of the gospel is available to them.

One of the greatest of Carey's achievements was the harassing of Government after Government until at last the killing of children, the burning alive of widows, and the burial alive of lepers were made criminal offences.

Little recognition came to Carey in his lifetime. No British university honoured him, it was left to an American university to make him a Doctor. But when he died in 1834, the Government that had fought him all his life lowered its flags.

To a visitor who came to see him as he was dying, and who spoke much of " Dr. Carey," Carey said, " When I am gone, say nothing about Dr. Carey, speak of Carey's Saviour." On his tomb, at his express wish, there is no mention of his achievements, but just this :

> A wretched, poor, and helpless worm,
> On Thy kind arms I fall.

Humble?—yes. A little man of poor physique?—yes; and yet a flame; dynamite; a saint—one of the saints through whom the nations now walk in the light. Carey's name is written in large letters across

Indian history. All that he did, all that has followed from his labours, defies summary. His fidelity and his enthusiasm will remain for ever an inspiration to others.

" It is in the missionary meeting that you may hear the beating of the Baptist heart."

Anon. Saying quoted by Dr. H. Wheeler Robinson *in " The Life and Faith of the Baptists."*

CHAPTER SIX

Those Who Bore the Torch

IT was the arrival of John Thomas from Bengal that drew Carey to India, and it was that beginning, and the peculiar interest England had in India, which led all the first missionary recruits to Carey's side. But it was soon felt that the Society must launch out further. Attention was turned first to Jamaica, a very flourishing colony with a Negro population. The first Baptist church in Jamaica had been founded, in 1784, by a Negro preacher from Georgia, but the church needed the services of an English missionary. It was, however, eight years before an Englishman arrived, and then he had many difficulties and much opposition to contend with. The first man to make any impression on the island was Coulthard, from Bristol College. The

outstanding man in the history of Jamaica
is William Knibb.

*   *   *   *

William Knibb was baptised by Dr.
Ryland, and two years later, in 1824, he
sailed for Jamaica. He followed his
brother Tom, who had gone to Jamaica as
a missionary some three months before, but
who had died after those very brief months
of service. William was deliberately taking
his brother's place. In those days slavery
was still flourishing in British Colonies, and
Knibb was horrified by what he saw. His
antagonism to this great evil brought him
opposition. The planters were not slow in
seeing that this young man was a keen
foe, and that his mission, which was
gathering converts by the thousand, was
likely to be dangerous to them. Knibb
was summoned before the House of
Assembly, and was finally thrown into
prison. The charges against him came to
nothing, but his life was in constant danger,
and his church buildings were destroyed.
It seemed that the twenty years of

missionary work had been useless, and the sacrifices had been in vain. The churches were wrecked, the schools dissolved, and laws were passed preventing any kind of missionary work.

Knibb did the only thing possible; he returned to England with the deliberate intention of setting the facts before the country. The Reform Bill of that year had awakened public opinion. The people were ready for Knibb.

The Committee of the Missionary Society was careful to enjoin upon Knibb the need for caution in stating his case. But Knibb was full of fire. He told his audiences that slavery and missions were incompatible: "Whatever the consequences, I *will* speak. At the risk of my connection with the Society, and all I hold dear, I will avow this—that if the friends of missions will not hear me I will turn and tell it to my God; nor will I desist until this greatest of curses, slavery, is removed, and 'Glory to God in the highest' inscribed on the British flag!"

Knibb, with his fellow-missionary,

Burchell, told the annual meeting of the Society that year (1833) how patient had been the conduct of the Negroes during the disturbances and the persecution. They told of the purity of their faith, and the endurance and courage they had shown.

Deep feeling was aroused in those who heard these stories. Knibb's speeches were greeted with deafening applause. The excitement spread through the Baptist churches, and resolutions were passed at all the meetings demanding that the slaves should be freed by the Government. Knibb had great powers of oratory, and his tour of the land became a triumphal procession. Thirteen thousand pounds were subscribed for the rebuilding of the wrecked churches. The Bill for the Abolition of Slavery was at last passed and, on Emancipation Day, Knibb heard the shout of joy that arose from the dusky multitudes. He was rewarded. Through his instrumentality the Africa that had been tragically wronged for centuries, bled almost white by the slave trade, had come to the dawn of a new era.

The honour of being the pioneers in the

movement for the abolition of slavery belongs to the Society of Friends, but Knibb led the Baptist contribution to that tide of public feeling which resulted in the abolition. The Baptist passion for liberty is a strongly marked characteristic; from their very beginning Baptists have always been in the forefront of the battle for political and religious liberty—as their place in Cromwell's Army clearly shows.

From Emancipation Day the energies of Knibb and his fellows were directed towards the saving and the lifting of the Africa they had helped to free.

Another field of the Baptist Missionary Society's work was the Cameroons. In 1845 the first Baptist mission station on the continent of Africa was established by Alfred Saker. Saker was the son of a Kentish wheelwright, and was working in the Government dockyard at Devonport when he offered himself for missionary work. He was a man of keen mind, able to use his hands (the first real impression made on the natives was the fact that Saker's home-made bricks could resist the onslaught of white ants,) and his spirit was deeply religious. He has been called " the Apostle of the Cameroons." Saker landed there in 1840 with a party of freed slaves from Jamaica; he purchased ten miles of coast, and named it Victoria. There he and his company settled, building their own homes; and there Saker laboured, and translated the Bible into the Duala language. On the transfer of the Cameroons to Germany in 1884, the work was taken over by German missionaries, but not before a new opening for the work of the Baptist Missionary Society in Africa had been found through the discovery of the Congo River. This leads to the story of the second great field of Baptist missionary enterprise.

*　　*　　*　　*

The Congo river is one of the wonders of the world. For thousands of years it has flowed right across Africa, but until fifty years ago the full extent of it was not known. Its outlet had long been known. Along its banks were many native fishing villages, but these knew only their own stretch of river: none knew where that great river came from. Livingstone had explored parts of it, but not until a white man appeared on August 2, 1877, at Nsanda, was the mystery solved. That man's name was Stanley, and he had traced the river across Africa.

Now while Henry Morton Stanley was pressing his way down the river, a miser was poring over the map of Africa in England. Robert Arthington had inherited a large fortune from his father. His father had been a brewer who had shut down his works in the very year Robert was born, being convinced that it was an iniquitous trade. Robert inherited from him some £200,000 and, being something of a financial genius, he turned that fortune into the bigger one of over £1,000,000. At the same time he became the traditional miser, going about Leeds in threadbare clothes, living on 2/6 a week, in a bare room as cold as ice. This eccentric dreamer, poring over maps of Africa in his bare room, not even daring to light a candle because of the cost, conceived the idea that the Congo river did indeed sweep right across Africa. He was passionately interested in missionary enterprise, and he saw that if the Congo river went across Africa it opened up that land to the missionaries. So he left the bulk of his fortune to the Baptist Missionary Society, which had the largest portion, and the London Missionary Society; while several other societies benefited. Each had to spend the money in twenty-five years, and each had to advance into Africa from a different corner. The miser's million has now done its work, and the chain of stations is complete; but at what a cost, in men, in suffering, in anxiety! It seemed at first as if every volunteer who went to Congo under the B.M.S. went to his death. Grenfell, Comber, Holman Bentley, Crudgington, Hartland were the first volunteers. Grenfell and Comber were the leaders. Hartland was the first of the tired toilers to be struck down. Malaria was their deadly foe. Congo became known as the short cut to heaven; at home it was even suggested that no more recruits should be sent; but there was an average of twelve volunteers ready to step into each vacant post. In five months of one year six missionaries fell. After nine years of service, Thomas Comber passed to his rest. The story of these years is a tragic one. In the first forty years of B.M.S. work on the Congo there were sixty-one deaths, but then gradually new methods of protection were discovered, until today the Congo is as safe as most other mission fields.

The sacrifice of the martyrs was not in vain. Their purpose was to establish a chain of stations all along the mighty river. For this a steamer was necessary, and the *Peace* was built for Grenfell in 1881. Engineers were sent from England to assemble the component parts but they died before they could do so. Grenfell, who had set all his hopes on the steamer, was baffled. Then at last, with the aid of a few native carpenters, he assembled it himself—a Midlander, with nothing but a theological training! By the end of 1890 the steamer had helped to open stations at Bolobo, Lukolela, Monsembe and Upoto. What do these names mean? They mean that where once were burning villages, as a result of slave raids, where there was once ignorance and vice, there was now light and love—the Gospel with all its transforming power.

Grenfell's part in the work was known to a wider public than that of any of his fellow-pioneers—and rightly so. His services to civilisation were of no common order, and won for him a considerable share of public honour. He was one of the greatest of Christian ambassadors, and one of the most brilliant pioneers of the age.

Grenfell was born near Penzance in 1849. He was educated at King Edward's School, Birmingham. At fifteen he dedicated his whole life to Christ. For some few years after leaving school he was in business, and then he entered the Baptist College at Bristol. At twenty-five he went to the Cameroons under the B.M.S., and four years later he went to the Congo.

Few men have ever loved Africa as George Grenfell did, and few understood it as well as he. Print cannot convey an adequate impression of this large-souled, sensitive, brilliant leader of the work on the Congo through so many perilous years. His was a nature sweetly tempered, gentle and kindly, of rich genius. He was a pioneer in every sense, a geographer and explorer, a wonderful linguist; with one thought foremost always—to open up Africa to the Gospel. Long before the project seemed feasible he had mapped out the long chain of mission stations.

One of the most memorable discoveries of Grenfell, as an explorer, was the course of the Mobangi, the northern tributary of the Congo. He explored territory after territory of Africa through the years, and acquired a great reputation as a geographer. And yet with great modesty he refused to exploit his discoveries, and so did not receive some of the honours his work deserved. The greatest honour he was given was the Founder's Medal of the Royal Geographical Society. Dr. Scott Keltie (Secretary of the Royal Geographical Society), writing after his death, said that Grenfell " deserves to be placed in the first rank among African explorers, not only for the extent of ground which he covered, and the accuracy of his work as a surveyor and cartographer, but also for the richness and value of his observations on the countries and their peoples through which he travelled, and among whom he sojourned." And again he said : " Had Mr. Grenfell been bent on fame and money-making he might have been one of the best known travellers of his time."

In 1906, George Grenfell was occupying in loneliness the last of the Congo mission stations, opened by himself only a few months before. He was waiting for others —a schoolmaster and evangelists—to join him there, at Yalemba. There he was suddenly laid up with fever, far removed from medical aid, and from his friends. His faithful native servants put their sick master on board the old steamer that had served him so well through the years, and brought him to Basoko, sending on word to the staff at Yakusu. So, through the care and love of his natives, he had his friends around him at the last, and was ministered to with deep devotion. The help had come too late, and on July 1, 1906,

George Grenfell died at the age of fifty-seven. *The Times* spoke of him as " an Englishman of almost incredible industry, unblemished reputation, and imperishable fame."

The whole of the Baptist churches mourned the loss of one worthy to be ranked with Livingstone and the other heroes whose names must ever be recalled when Africa is discussed.

Holman Bentley must also be mentioned. He was a pioneer in linguistic work on the Congo languages. He was a son of the manse, and proved to be an original thinker, and a fine scholar. From the beginning of his settlement in the country he set himself to study the language with a view to reducing it to a literary and scientific form. The fruit of his scholarship was a Congo Dictionary, Grammar, New Testament, and a partially completed Old Testament.

So the story goes on. The missionaries pressed some thirteen hundred miles up the Congo. The result is that, where there was once fear and devilry, cannibal feasts and domestic slavery, there are now in the fifteen B.M.S. areas some two thousand eight hundred organised congregations and some twenty-three thousand church members. The Gospel, taught by those pioneers, has wrought a marvellous change in the lives of the people. King Albert of the Belgians, writing in 1928, said of this work: " It is my sincere wish that this civilising work may develop still further in the years to come."

It is almost impossible to exaggerate the interest this Congo story, as it was gradually unfolded, aroused in the Baptist churches. Churches were prepared to give most generously in those days, when death and disaster seemed the only return; but the story was an heroic one. In it there is a wealth of material for the student of missionary enterprise. The conspicuous leaders have been selected for mention in this résumé of the story, but the same spirit marked all the missionaries. In the story of the Congo mission there is a revelation of heroism and greatness which is inspiring. Some of the eager volunteers who pressed into the gaps in the ranks served but a few months, but the spirit of the lowliest was as ardent and as deserving of honour as that of the best known. There was a dynamic in their lives at least as great as that which sent out romantic heroes like Drake to quest and conquest.

*   *   *   *

The third great area to be entered by Baptist missionaries was Northern China. Work began with the arrival of Timothy Richard in Shantung in 1870. Richard's name remains the outstanding one in this field.

Timothy Richard was the son of a blacksmith in a remote Welsh village, a village to which neither newspaper nor train penetrated. The blacksmith's family was large, and his children had to fend for themselves as soon as they could. Timothy was denied every opportunity that comes to boys to-day; he had to gain his education in devious ways, in the course of which he borrowed every book in the village. He was baptised in the open river, like Bunyan, Carey, Knibb, Spurgeon, Clifford, and Lloyd George. He preached his first sermon in

Timothy Richard,
1845-1919.

the village chapel, and from there went to
the College at Haverfordwest. His great
ambition was to be a missionary to China,
and at last this shy lad from Wales, looking
more like a farmer than a student, faced
the B.M.S. Committee. He was slow in
speech, and the awful presence of the great
men of the denomination froze him into
silence. The Committee, in consequence,
nearly rejected him, and it was this
possibility that aroused him.

"Suppose we reject you, Mr. Richard,
what will you do?" they said. "Go to
China," was the calm reply. "But, my
dear sir, how?" they asked. "Swim," was
the laconic answer, and the startled Committee accepted him!

Richard was a far-sighted man, a genius
in many ways, universal in mind and in
heart. He looked for a point of contact in
every man he met, and, finding seekers after
God everywhere, he won them for his Christ.
In those early days, over fifty years ago, he
was preaching a social Gospel. He loved
all new inventions, and played with them
like a large-hearted boy with a new toy;

he used them to extend his Master's Kingdom. He wrote leading articles for the great newspapers of China. He cultivated the friendship of the prominent Chinese leaders. He was behind the Reform Movement of 1898, and many experts have paid their tribute to him as the one man who did more than any other man to reform China. He was prominent in the organisation of relief in the great famine of 1876-1878. Such a list only touches the fringe of his activities, however.

In 1900 the Boxer Rising took place, and 200 missionaries were martyred, but in the reaction three Governors of Provinces appealed to Richard for advice and help. *The Times* reported this, and said of Richard that " his personal influence with the literati is largely due to his broad and generous sympathy with the best aspects of Chinese thought." The result of the reaction was that Shansi was fined £60,000, with which the Government founded Shansi University. Richard was put in charge as Chancellor.

Richard laid special stress on the importance of Christian literature in missionary work, and was made secretary of the Christian Literature Society. The position he held in the esteem of the peoples of China is seen in the fact that, when he returned in 1910 to China from England, the President of the Provincial Assembly of Shansi sent him an urgent telegram inviting him to an official reception, and informing him that the session of the Assembly would be extended for five days in order to welcome him. He was received at the railway station by the President, the Vice-Presidents, and the representatives of the Assembly. The imagination is delighted with this picture of a Prime Minister receiving a Baptist minister at the railway station.

Richard was an idealist and a dreamer but not an impractical one. In 1905 he dreamed of a federation of ten of the leading countries of the world. The dream was scorned, but after the tragedy of the first World War (1914-18) the nations formed such a league. He also pleaded for the reform of missionary methods; he said that " natives can best influence their fellow-

countrymen to join the Christian Church."
Carey had seen that too, and modern
missionary methods are giving more and
more time to the training and oversight of
native teachers and leaders, and the native
is being left free to interpret Christian faith
in his own way. The dreamer, then, was a
great practical leader, and his work and influence helped to change a nation of
400,000,000 souls.

*   *   *   *

In Burma, where Judson the American
Baptist worked, there is a memorial to him
which is also a symbol of all missionary
work. The palace of the King, under whom
Judson suffered, has long ago crumbled to
ruins; the palaces of the native grandees
have disappeared; the foul prison in which
that gallant missionary suffered terrible
horrors has gone. But where that prison
stood is a memorial, a huge granite block,
on which is inscribed the simple record that
here stood the prison in which the
missionary suffered indescribable terrors.
That is significant: the glory of kings

departs, ancient tyrannies vanish, the service of the missionary and the triumph of the Cross survive all changes.

" In this gathering to-night . . almost every land upon earth is represented. This is a dream which even Bunyan never had in Bedford Gaol. . . . We have come together here, the representatives of a vast community, trying to keep in their simplicity both the symbolic ordinances of Christ, and to do whatsoever He has commanded, until He come."

The REV. J. H. SHAKESPEARE, M.A., *Secretary of the First Baptist World Congress, 1905, at the Inaugural Meeting.*

CHAPTER SEVEN
GREAT ADMINISTRATORS

SO far the heroes of the Baptist Church have been portrayed as they come into view in the gradual development of that Church. Now space must be devoted to certain men who have not come fully into any of the previous chapters. The Baptist Church owes much to men who were administrators more than they were anything else. This is not to suggest that they were not evangelists and teachers also, they were passionately concerned in the establishment of the Kingdom, but they served that cause primarily as administrators.

*　　*　　*　　*

It is first necessary to go back to the early days of the Puritan cause. By the year 1617 the Separatist exiles who had remained in Holland—the original group from Gainsborough had been joined by other groups in the intervening years—began to realise that Holland could not be their abiding home. It had been a useful refuge, but the fear that the colony might become a permanent part of the Dutch population caused the leaders to think of seeking refuge elsewhere. No place offered such advantages as Virginia, and it was at last decided to ask leave to settle there. Leave was granted in 1619. The next urgent business was to find and provision two or more ships. The *Speedwell* and the *Mayflower* were secured, and in August, 1620, the two ships sailed from Southampton. Twice, however, on flimsy excuses, the captain of the *Speedwell* put back. At last the *Speedwell* was left behind, and the pilgrims all set sail in the *Mayflower*. When they finally sighted land, they found that they were far from Virginia, but they brought the *Mayflower* into what is now Plymouth Harbour. Thus the Pilgrim Fathers established themselves in America. Their little colony was founded on the principles of John Smyth.* The original settlement soon was surpassed by others. A group settled at Providence, and here, in 1639, Roger Williams was baptised. To Roger Williams is owed the founding of the first Baptist church in America.

Williams was a Welshman, born about the beginning of the 17th century. He was educated at Charterhouse, and entered as a student to Cambridge in 1623. He graduated from Pembroke College in 1626. There is little to indicate that he actually became a lawyer, although he is supposed to have studied law at Cambridge, but he did become a very acceptable preacher. In 1629 he was chaplain to Sir W. Masham, in Essex. He held an extreme Puritan position, and because of it was exiled. He sailed with his wife from Bristol in the *Lion,* on December 1, 1630. He landed at Boston, and was soon invited to be one of the pastors there. This church did not seem, to his mind, to have renounced sufficiently all connection with the Church of England, so he refused the

* See *Smith the Se-Baptist,* by Burgess, pp. 338ff, for a good account of the Pilgrim Fathers.

honour. For some time he ministered in Plymouth. Williams at this time seems to have been headstrong and tactless. The Puritans had gone to the New World to escape persecution, but not necessarily to grant religious liberty to all who came with them. Williams incurred their anger, and he was accordingly banished. The months that followed were romantic enough to suit a present-day film-producer on the look-out for material. Williams wandered for long as an outcast; he was sheltered by savage tribes, he tried to found a settlement on the Pawtucket River and failed, but finally he settled near the mouth of the Mohassuck River, where he founded the town of Providence. It is a good testimony to his character that many of his old church members followed him. He bought land and maintained a city of refuge for the persecuted, setting up and administering a democratic State in which complete religious freedom was allowed to all. That is his great achievement.

Williams became a Baptist; in 1639 he appointed a member of the church to baptise him, and then he baptised the rest. Thus the first Baptist church on American soil was founded.

Williams obtained a charter for his settlement, and his State prospered under his wise leadership. His character was such that even his former foes came to admire him. In 1644 he visited England, no longer a rash exile, but the father of his Colony, and the exponent of a new theory of government—a true democracy, with complete religious toleration. Williams said of his Colony: "Out of this seed shall arise the most glorious Commonwealth known to human history." His dream was not a foolish one, for that ideal of religious toleration was accepted as a fundamental part of the Constitution of the United States of America.

* * * *

The second great Baptist administrator came from a little ramshackle farmhouse in Cambridgeshire. He was born in 1754, and began work on the farm at ten years of age. He had to rough it, with few amusements or pleasures. The small and bare Baptist church where his parents worshipped was not likely to be an inspiration to such a lad: its seats were hard and its theology harder. Its theology was the extreme Calvinism of the period: that is to say, it maintained that a favoured few were arbitrarily selected by God for eternal life, while the rest were eternally damned. The minister of the church, in such circumstances, naturally had little to say, except to believers, and (according to this lad, in later life) he never even explained what believing was. That narrow Calvinism nearly robbed the Kingdom of a great hero, and the Baptist Missionary Society of the greatest administrator in the whole of its history: the lad's name was Andrew Fuller.

During Andrew Fuller's boyhood, the Evangelical Revival was slowly breaking down the hard, narrow Calvinism of the churches. Among Baptists, Robert Hall was preaching a practical evangelism. The changing mood was to be seen in Ralph Erskine's *Gospel Sonnets,* and somehow they reached the Cambridgeshire fens. These sonnets were concerned with the free love of God and, through them, Andrew Fuller found a Saviour. Something else happened too, which meant much to him: a fellow-member of the little church was found drunk, and Andrew Fuller rebuked him. The church was horrified at the rebuke, and Andrew Fuller only escaped censure on the score of his youth. He was told that it was God's business to save His children from sinning, and that it was presumption for him to interfere. But Andrew Fuller had a conscience, and he could not reconcile his conscience with such a narrow theology. So the lad of sixteen began to remould his theology and, amid the fens of Cambridgeshire, he was guided by the Spirit. By the time Fuller sought to enter college he had written a book, *The Gospel worthy of all Acceptation.* He did not publish it until he became pastor at Kettering, but even then the theologians of the denomination were very much disturbed by this manifesto of a new theology: no, not a new theology,

8

a rediscovery of the eternal Gospel. The Gospel was breaking through the rigid system of theology men had built up, a system which had long been shackling the churches.

Fuller had not seen the logical outcome of his work, but there was a shoemaker named William Carey not far away, who also cared nothing for the rigid Calvinism of the day but everything for the heathen. It is remarkable that when a new discovery has been due to break upon the world it has often been revealed to two men at once. Adams and Leverrier made a simultaneous discovery of the planet Neptune. Edison and Swan invented the electric lamp almost together. The names of Darwin and Wallace also stand together. The discovery is made doubly sure by being revealed to two. So it was that, when missions were in the mind of God, Fuller was inspired to write his book and Carey to make his globe of small pieces of shoe leather. It ended by Carey volunteering as the first missionary, and Fuller organising a society to support Carey.

Rev. Andrew Fuller

1754-1815.

Fuller was a remarkable secretary. He had no office but his own study. He had no missionaries home on furlough to send on deputation work, he had to do all that himself. He had a fine Committee to back him, it is true; but he told them, "I will consult you, for you are wiser than I; but I am more courageous. . . . I will execute without you." He had little money to spare, and he received no salary from the Society. He was always having to tackle problems, and he was always trying to get money out of those who had it but did not want to part with it. He raised the money. The Serampore Press was burned down, but in six weeks Fuller collected the funds needed to rebuild it. He toiled twelve hours a day at his desk. At other times he travelled night and day, often for long hours without sleep and without food. His wife said, with tears in her eyes, "You have no time to talk to me. You will be worn out soon." "I know it," was the brave reply, "but I cannot be worn out in a better cause."

Fuller was an unassuming hero, a brave

fighter, a humble, self-denying disciple. He sustained and led the missionary passion of the Baptists, leading it into the right channels. It was his loyal devotion, his untiring energy, and his wise administration which helped to make the Baptist Missionary Society famous. He died, worn out, at the age of sixty-one years.

*　　　*　　　*　　　*

Forty-six years after the death of Andrew Fuller a new statesman came to the service of the B.M.S. In the records of the Society there is this entry, dated February 11, 1861 : " Resolved that Mr. A. Baynes, in conformity with the recommendation of the Finance Committee, be appointed to the office of accountant."

Mr. Baynes was a young man of twenty-two years of age, in the employ of the Treasurer of the B.M.S.—Sir S. Morton Peto. It had been found that the book-keeping of the Society needed expert attention, and Sir Morton Peto had lent this young man to do the work. It seemed an unimportant step, but in later years Sir

Morton Peto used to say that the best gift he had ever made to the Society was the gift of his own secretary—Mr. A. H. Baynes. Some nine years after his first appointment, he was asked to add to his duties those of minute secretary. Another six years passed and he was then appointed co-secretary, and finally sole general secretary of the B.M.S. In that office he was destined to serve for some twenty-seven years. To that office he gave his best gifts —and they were considerable. He was in every way a statesman, a great administrator. He was always alert to recognise new opportunities, and ever ready to kindle the enthusiasm needed to take full advantage of them. The flame of his own enthusiastic nature kindled a like flame in the hearts of others. With faith, courage, devotion, and tireless patience, he led the fortunes of the B.M.S. brilliantly during his years of office.

To many—who heard his challenging and intensely inspiring speeches, or received his gracious letters—Alfred Henry Baynes, J.P. *was* the Baptist Missionary Society.

This able secretary had all the details of the Society at his finger tips. He was very shrewd in his judgments, sound on financial problems, and in everything utterly consecrated to God's service. All who had to deal with him found him considerate and sympathetic; they found the Christian behind the official.

Certain simple facts sum up his work. When he entered upon the secretaryship there were less than forty missionaries in India and only two in China. When he retired there were seventy-three in India and over thirty in China. When he began his work there was an annual gross income of some £46,000, and when he retired that sum was nearly doubled every year. These facts give some idea of the growth of the Society, and that growth is attributable, under God, to A. H. Baynes.

With hardly an exception the missionaries of the Society loved their general secretary. When in trouble or difficulty it was his help they sought and they never sought in vain. He took every possible opportunity of furthering their welfare and was an adept at surreptitiously slipping a bank-note into a hand when he knew how welcome it would be in some difficult circumstance. To them all he was not an official but a friend and a brother. He was a layman whose labours were apostolic.

The ministry of the layman is fully maintained and jealously asserted amongst Baptists. There is nothing which a minister is called upon to do which a layman is theoretically debarred from doing. From the earliest days Baptists have asserted this, although they have never had any highly organised system of lay preachers such as the Methodists. In the early days of Baptist history there was no professional ministry, the butcher or the baker laid down his tools, when he felt so called, and travelled over his county.

The Baptist churches can never repay the debt they owe to such laymen. Helwys, Murton, Allen, were all laymen. Thomas Guy, the Baptist Bible-printer, put more than a denomination in his debt when he devoted his fortune of £220,000 to founding a hospital that is still a blessing to London. The service of gifted laymen was not confined to England, The names of such men as Collett of Madras and General Havelock of India stand out. And Alfred Henry Baynes was a notable addition to the long list of laymen who have rendered great service to the denomination.

It may be fairly claimed that the emphasis upon missionary activity is a characteristic of the Baptist churches, and the Missionary Society that Mr. Baynes did so much for now fills a very large corner of their hearts. Its achievements during his administration can be compared by no means unfavourably with that of other denominations with greater resources of men and money.

In 1906 Mr. Baynes retired from the active administration of the affairs of the Society, but he rendered many valuable services until his death in 1914.

*　　*　　*　　*

It is noticeable that gradually (coinciding with the time of organisation and expansion

JOHN HOWARD SHAKESPEARE,
1857-1928

in the Missionary Society) the churches on the home front increased and strengthened their organisation. In 1863 it was decided, because of the growing corporate spirit, and the rapid advancement of the Baptist cause, to appoint a Secretary for the whole country. Since then great attention has been paid to organisation. Societies have been linked, Associations have been strengthened, and an administration has taken shape.

A new force, a great administrator, arose in the Baptist Church when John Howard Shakespeare came to the chair of Secretary. Dr. Shakespeare, whose biography has yet to be written, was a statesman, an administrator with vision. He came as Secretary to a Baptist Union which rented three rooms from the B.M.S. at 19, Furnival Street; to a Union which had little real cohesion, with but a tiny income. He convinced the denomination that dreams could be achieved. He produced the plans, his genius lifted the plans out of the ruts of routine, he toured the country and one by one his dreams came true. Fund after fund was raised; he launched the Baptist

Church House upon its career, giving the denomination a centre and a home. The Baptist Church owes much to his fertile brain.

John Howard Shakespeare was a son of the manse. The Rev. Benjamin Shakespeare held pastorates at Liverpool (where he rendered very brave service during a cholera epidemic), Kilham, and Malton. Here his second son, John Howard, was born on April 16, 1857. Benjamin Shakespeare retired from the ministry soon after, and settled first at Derby, then at Leicester. In each town the family joined the nearest Baptist church. The church at Belvoir Street, Leicester, was the scene of the ministry of the Rev. J. P. Mursell. The Rev. James Thew was assistant minister, and it was under his influence that John gradually turned his thoughts towards the ministry. His aspirations were enthusiastically received by his parents.

For some time Shakespeare worked in an insurance office in London, gaining a knowledge of business methods which was to be invaluable later. In London he was baptised by Dr. Landels, and joined his church at Regent's Park. He still wanted to enter the ministry. Dr. Landels was a member of the Committee of Regent's Park College; Dr. Angus, the Principal, was also a member of the church. The way was therefore opened very easily for Shakespeare to enter college. He had a brilliant academic career, graduating M.A. with honours in philosophy. Towards the end of his college course he was sent by Dr. Angus as a supply to St. Mary's Church, Norwich. The pastorate of the church was vacant at the time, the Rev. George Gould having just died. Neither Dr. Angus, nor the young student, imagined that the visit was anything but an opportunity for gaining preaching experience. St. Mary's is one of oldest and greatest churches in the denomination, having had a long succession of able and distinguished ministers. On its diaconate were some of the City Fathers and leading business men of the town. These recognised the out-

standing ability of the youthful preacher.
An enthusiastic invitation to the pastorate
was given him, and with some misgivings
he accepted it. In 1883 Shakespeare was
ordained as minister of the church.

The position Shakespeare occupied was
not without its perils and its difficulties.
St. Mary's was a " down-town" church,
old-fashioned seating shut worshippers into
narrow straight-backed " cells "; and the
congregation had also begun to dwindle in
the interval between Gould's death and the
arrival of Shakespeare. However, Shakespeare brought new life and enthusiasm to
the church. His preaching was vivid,
dramatic and arresting. The wanderers
returned to the fold; newcomers forgot the
hard, narrow, cell-like pews in their enjoy-
ment of this great preacher. Fresh
organisations were born; the church
buildings were altered, and the cost of the
renovations was met before the close of the
reopening services.

The denomination was not slow in
realising that a brilliant preacher and
thinker had been found by St. Mary's in

this young man fresh from college. In 1884 he appeared on the platform of the Baptist Union and gave an address on "Truths Essential to Church Prosperity." Later he preached a striking sermon for the Missionary Society. And then, at the Assembly held in London in 1892, he gave an address on "Baptist Church Extension in Large Towns." That address, brilliant and sound in argument, as well as original and audacious, captured the attention of the denomination. Here, it was recognised, was a statesman with insight and ability, shrewd in judgment, sound in faith.

In 1898 Dr. Booth, the Secretary of the Baptist Union, resigned. The Council at once turned to Shakespeare. After difficulties, owing to an illness, he accepted nomination for the office, and was elected by the Assembly held that year at Nottingham. In his speech acknowledging election to office he gave several hints as to the aims he would set himself: he mentioned the promotion of Church Extension; the quickening of the denominational conscience; and the lifting of the burdens of humble village ministers. Those were more than hints, they were prophecies. For twenty-six years he occupied his important office, and he fulfilled each of his dreams.

The Baptist Union was altogether subordinate to the Missionary Society, being a poor tenant in that Society's fine house, with delegates who were paid their travelling expenses by the B.M.S.; and it was only able to call meetings at the convenience of the Society. The income of the Union was £18,390 in the year Shakespeare took office, and of that sum £10,084 was interest on the invested capital of the Annuity Fund coupled with the premiums of the members.

Shakespeare had to face big problems and to carry heavy burdens during the opening years of his secretaryship. The first task he set his hand to was the raising of £250,000. The Assembly which had appointed him to office had suggested raising such a sum to mark the passage from the 19th to the 20th century. One half of it was to be used for Church Extension and the other half for various denominational objects—one of which Shakespeare decided must be to build a Church House worthy of the denomination. Shakespeare's first task was to convince the churches that such a sum was not an impossible one. Then he had to create an organisation capable of raising and distributing it. The ability he brought to these tasks places him in the front rank of Baptist heroes and leaders. Shakespeare was always able to inspire others with his own confidence and enthusiasm. He was a born leader, and he was fortunate in having with him as Presidents men like Dr. Clifford, William Cuff, and Dr. Maclaren. Ably backed by the rank and file, Shakespeare overcame all difficulties, and was able to announce in 1902 that the Fund was complete. It was typical of Shakespeare that, in a day when it was unseemly for a woman to take part in a church meeting, or even to pray in a prayer meeting, he enlisted the women of the denomination in raising this Fund.

For the next few years Shakespeare was engaged in improving the internal organisation of the Baptist Union. He had also to administer the Twentieth Century

Fund now that it was completed. It was not an easy task to apportion the £125,000 set aside for Church Extension, there were competing claims from different parts of the country. But by 1906 some 75 new churches had been built by means of the Fund.

The Baptist Church House was one of Shakespeare's dreams: that dream, too, came true through the Twentieth Century Fund, and the denomination now owns its dignified and commodious Church House in Southampton Row.

In 1905 the first Baptist World Congress was held in London. The idea originated from America, but it was Shakespeare who undertook the immense organisation necessary to carry it through. Four thousand delegates attended from all parts of the world, the Baptist leaders in every country being present. Something of the organisation which had been going on, not merely in England, but all over the world, was revealed when it was shown that the Baptist Communion was represented on every continent, and had become one of the largest, if not *the* largest, of the Protestant bodies. It was Shakespeare's administrative vigour that made the Baptist Union, and then this Baptist World Alliance, effective organisations; he laid down foundations upon which the denomination and the Alliance have built for years.

The second great problem that Shakespeare had to face was that of the status of the ministry. Many of the leaders of the denomination were already thinking of a Sustentation Fund. One was working very successfully in the Presbyterian Church. But Shakespeare saw that, before a great Fund could be raised to help ministers in poor churches, the whole question of the status and recognition of ministers must be considered. A scheme of Ministerial Recognition was necessary as a preliminary to a Sustentation scheme. After much controversy a scheme of Ministerial Recognition was finally accepted in 1911. The next year it was resolved to raise a Sustentation Fund of £250,000. Having built up an organisation for the purpose of raising the Twentieth Century Fund,

Shakespeare knew what lines to follow now. Again he appealed to the women (in 1908 he had founded a Baptist Women's League), and he asked them to raise £50,000. Inspired by Shakespeare, they proceeded to raise £60,000. The Sustentation Fund grew steadily. Shakespeare's eloquent and persuasive tongue was irresistible. When the Fund was closed it had reached £285,000.

When the first Great War came it was realised that Baptists and Congregationalists were without chaplains in the Army. The War Office recognised five "religions": Roman Catholics, Anglicans, Presbyterians, Wesleyans, and Jews were all catered for. Everyone else was outside the pale. The War Office turned a deaf ear to all protests, it had no use for "queer sects." But Shakespeare was Shakespeare, and he also had some influential friends. The result was a United Board of Nonconformists, with the right of nominating chaplains to care for their own men. These chaplains had equal rights with Anglicans.

After the 1914-1918 War the denomination was faced with grave difficulties.

Great numbers of ministers were reduced to poverty, churches were on the verge of collapse. The B.M.S., too, was facing grave financial troubles owing to the rise in exchange. It was agreed, therefore, to raise a further fund of £250,000, to be divided between the Baptist Union and the B.M.S. This time the land was divided into Association areas, with a Committee and Commissioners in charge of each. This United Fund was raised with ease, and reached £273,000. The Union was able, through the Fund, to raise the minimum salary of ministers. To help ministers and their wives was the delight of Shakespeare. He deplored the need, but he was delighted that this and his previous Fund eased the financial situation in many a manse. He raised these great Funds with such ease because he made people believe in their possibility. £70,000 of the United Fund was contributed by the women of the denomination. Shakespeare believed very emphatically in enlisting the women in the work of the churches. He used to say: " The essential difference between a committee of men and one of women is that the men meet to decide upon what the Secretary is to do, and the women meet to decide upon what they are going to do." Through him representation upon the Baptist Union Council was opened to women.

Shakespeare had one great dream which never came to fulfilment. His desire for Christian reunion was a great passion. Both sides misunderstood him, and he was often attacked by both friend and foe at once. Convictions and prejudices stood in his way, and he at last saw that any reunion of the Anglican and the Free Churches in England in his lifetime was impossible. Though he went further than many of his fellow-Baptists would have gone, Shakespeare stopped short at re-ordination: that he could not consent to. But if no positive results were achieved, a new spirit of fellowship and co-operation was in no small measure due to his efforts. And the Federal Council of the Free Churches— speaking with one voice upon Free Church matters—grew out of his labours.

Toward the end of his life, Shakespeare

suffered a great tragedy : he lost the sight of one eye. The thought that his work was done appalled him, and he grew very depressed. He resigned his office in 1925. At first it seemed as if he would not survive the depression that had laid hold of him. After a while he regained some of his old alertness and enthusiasm, and even lent a helping hand at the Church House; but suddenly he was struck down with paralysis. He was left helpless and speechless, but with little pain. He bore the monotony of the remaining days with great courage, passing away in March, 1928.

Shakespeare's married life was a very happy one. The lady whom Spurgeon called " the pastor's pastor " made his home life one of rich peace and happiness, without which he could not have carried out his exhausting labours.

Shakespeare refused the many honours that were offered him—with the exception of two, the honorary degrees of D.D. and LL.D. conferred upon him by Glasgow and McMaster Universities.

In summing up, it may be said that

Shakespeare came to the Baptist Union at a time when its organisation was very crude, and he left it with an efficient and highly organised administration able to meet all its needs. He raised Fund after Fund, although he was at first regarded as a well-meaning but irresponsible official. He had at first much to suffer from the sort of people who invariably discover the sinister activity of the Pope or the Devil in any attempt to do things in a new way. The story of the raising of the money for his great Funds would read like a romance if it could be fully told. Behind the enthusiasm that raised the money was a passionate desire to improve the ministry. Shakespeare realised that the Baptist Church depended upon the character and status of the man in the pulpit. Shakespeare's hard work, his mastery of intricate finance, his brilliant ingenuity, his tact, his close attention to detail, was directly responsible for the success of the great causes to which he set his hand. He was one of the ablest leaders the Free Churches have ever produced. No man without infinite vision, love, and enthusiasm could have done what he did. His life was spacious and noble, dedicated wholly to the Baptist Church and to its supreme Head.

"O zeal of Christ, seize us! absorb us! consume us! Give us no rest, night or day, except as we are saving our fellows and glorifying Thee!"

JOHN CLIFFORD.

JOHN CLIFFORD,
1836-1923.

CHAPTER EIGHT

"MR. GREATHEART" AND
"MR. VALIANT-FOR-TRUTH"

THERE is an embarrassing wealth of
material for the biographer and
historian of the Baptist Church. In this
short study, however, conspicuous leaders
have been selected here and there, and so
gradually the broad sketch of the denominational history has lengthened out almost to
modern times. Two heroes remain to be
considered: two great Baptists of modern
times who together sum up the Baptist
denomination. The whole of Baptist
history is to be found symbolised in the lives
of these two men—C. H. Spurgeon and
John Clifford. Here is the Baptist Great-
heart and here is Mr. Valiant-for-Truth.
Here is the one with his evangelistic ardour
and here the other with his democratic
passion. These two men are complemen-
tary; true evangelism and a deep passion

for liberty are but different aspects of the same truth and, through three hundred years of history, Baptists have held these principles dearer than life itself.

*   *   *   *

Charles Haddon Spurgeon was born in 1834, the second of ten children born to Pastor John Spurgeon and his wife. One child, among ten, in the home of a poor Congregational minister: it does not suggest a great career for that child. There was no State education in those days, the life of the poorer classes was very hard indeed. Two-thirds of the child population of the land were growing up without schooling; many were living amid brutal and immoral, over-crowded courts. Physical health was low. There was little to relieve the monotony of dismal lives amid mean streets and dark alleys. It was hard amid such conditions for the children of a poor family to rise above the rut, but John Spurgeon helped his children do it. For many years of his boyhood, Charles lived with his grandfather, the Congregational

CHARLES HADDON SPURGEON,
1834-1892.

minister at Stambourne. Afterwards he had schooling at Colchester and Maidstone and, in the autumn of 1849, he went as an articled pupil to a school in Newmarket. Up to the age of sixteen Spurgeon was restless, seeking in desperate earnestness a true way of life. Then, on the first Sunday in January, 1850, owing to a snowstorm, he was unable to get as far as he intended, and turned into a little Primitive Methodist church. There were about a dozen people present, the planned preacher was snowed up, and "a shoemaker, or tailor, or something of that sort" went up into the pulpit to preach. He took for his text, "Look unto me and be ye saved, all the ends of the earth"; he bungled the pronunciation, and he soon exhausted his thoughts. But it was then that he looked straight at Spurgeon and cried, "Young man, you look very miserable! You always will be miserable—miserable in life and miserable in death, if you don't obey my text: but if you obey now, this moment you will be saved. Young man, look to Jesus! Look! Look! Look! You have nothing to do but to look and live." The preaching was crude, but God has many strange servants, and the boy returned home with new faith in his heart. And from that moment he bore constant witness to Christ's saving power.

It was not long before Spurgeon was baptised. The cook in the school where he was an usher at Newmarket was a Baptist, and had a great influence over him; he said in later life that her conversation was better than the teaching of six doctors of divinity! She apparently led him to see the truth of the Baptist position, and he was baptised in the river Lark with two other disciples. His parents never accepted his Baptist views, but they raised no objections, though his mother wrote that she had often prayed that he might become a Christian but not that he might become a Baptist. With characteristic humour, Spurgeon replied that it was just like God not only to answer prayer but to do more than He was asked!

Presently Spurgeon moved to Cambridge; and there he began to preach, going out in all weathers to preach to the country audiences—sometimes in churches, and often in the open-air. He gained such a reputation as a preacher that he was soon called to the pulpit of Waterbeach; it was not a very promising village, but in a short while the change for the better was remarkable. Then, in a strange way, he received an invitation to preach in New Park Street pulpit, London. New Park Street was a famous church that had sadly deteriorated by 1853, and was then living on its past. Spurgeon's morning congregation was smaller than that of Waterbeach; however, his preaching brought out a much larger number in the evening, and they refused to go until the deacons had promised to invite him again. It is not surprising that he was later called to the pastorate of the church.

In 1854 Spurgeon's London pastorate began, and for thirty-eight years he preached to huge crowds in that city. His success began before either he or anyone else was fully aware of it, and from that moment the size of the crowds listening to him was only determined by the size of the building in which he preached. On the Day of National Humiliation for the Indian Mutiny he preached to 23,654 people in the Crystal Palace. Within a year the church at New Park Street had to be enlarged; but still it was too small, and for a while he preached at Exeter Hall, and then at the Royal Surrey Gardens Music Hall, (where something like eight thousand people could be accommodated). Many attacked him for holding religious services in a music hall, but he was not to be deterred. The great gatherings amazed London. In 1861 the Tabernacle, capable of holding more than five thousand, was erected at Newington Butts, then a growing suburb.

What was it that drew the crowds to this young preacher? He owed nothing to ceremonial; he stood before men very simply, in appearance he might have been a farmer. It is true he was humorous, and uncompromisingly original; he had a wonderful voice with which he took endless pains, and he had considerable histrionic gifts. But these qualities do not reveal the real secret of the man. He was a Greatheart, a large-souled man, liberal and loving, strong in faith, and passionately devoted to his Master. He towered above his fellows in many ways, most of all in spirit.

Spurgeon's achievements can be written in terms of the material: that is easy, and it makes a wonderful story. He built the Tabernacle, paid for it, and preached in it three times a week for many years to crowds that never grew less. He built his college for training young men for the ministry, a college which in the course of its history has trained over 1,300 men. Spurgeon's Orphanage was founded in response to the challenge of a generous lady who entrusted him with the necessary funds, and the Orphanage has received and educated and fathered some 5,000 children. His sermons fill sixty-six volumes, and he wrote a hundred other books. But this list of material achievements does not represent the real worth of the man. There have been in history but few religious leaders of creative genius; Spurgeon was one. His abiding achievement was not in building Tabernacle, or Orphanage, or College, but in changing the whole of life for so many thousands of people, and in recalling the Baptist Church to its true business—the conversion of men and women. He came to London in a day when a rigid Calvinism bound the churches, and without hesitation he set that hyper-Calvinism aside. In consequence he was attacked all his life by the strict Calvinists; yet he put evangelism in its true place. Spurgeon appealed to the moral conscience in each individual. In an age of doubt he preached hope and joy and peace through the grace of Jesus Christ. His teaching was not without a stern side; he taught that life was a serious business, and he could say some hard, stinging things to the smug and the complacent. He had an unshakeable faith in the truth of the Gospel he preached.

All his life Spurgeon suffered severely, but out of his own pain and suffering he learned to speak to others with infinite tenderness. His pain increased rapidly towards the end; his strength departed, and after great weakness and pain he died in France in 1892. A number of days passed before his body could be brought to London, and during those days it was remarkable how the thought of the civilised world centred on him and his work. At his funeral enormous crowds lined the roads.

The story is told of Spurgeon that, towards the end of his life, he was walking one day up Norwood Hill with a friend. Some distance ahead of them, moving up the hill, they could see a lamplighter, lighting lamp after lamp until he disappeared over the brow of the hill. Turning to his friend, Spurgeon said : " I hope my life will be just like that. I should like to think that when I've gone over the brow of the hill I shall leave lights shining behind me." Spurgeon left many lights behind him. More than any other great preacher he fashioned and moulded others after his own model. His influence will not leave the earth until they have all left it : perhaps not then. That is the greatest of all tributes to his ministry.

* * * *

Baptists, as has been seen again and again in these pages, have had two great passions

10

—for evangelism and for individual liberty. In John Smyth is heard the first explicit plea for liberty; Roger Willaims took the principle of complete religious freedom to America; Adjutant-General Allen, General Deane, Colonel Hutchinson, and others fought for the religious liberty so long denied them; William Knibb led the Baptist crusade against slavery. This line of Baptist crusaders was to culminate in John Clifford. C. H. Spurgeon was born ten days after Carey died; the evangelistic succession was maintained. John Clifford was nine years old when Knibb died; the succession of crusaders was assured.

In 1836, when John Clifford was born in a small Derbyshire village, industry was living on the life-blood of the workers. Boys and girls were as cogs in the pitiless factory machine, they worked twelve to sixteen hours a day under terrible conditions. Young Clifford joined them at nine years of age, becoming a "Jacker-off" in a lace factory at half-a-crown a week. At twelve years of age he was beginning work at four o'clock in the morning, and was receiving four shillings a week. He mixed with children who were hired at a cheap rate from the local workhouses. There were no trade unions to protect the workers, "hands" were cheap, and their cheapness was declared to be necessary for an industrial age. Nevertheless, those conditions have since been changed beyond recognition. Now much of the national income is devoted to social services, and the outstanding reforms of the past century have brought increasing dignity and freedom to the worker. John Clifford, the lad in the lace factory, stands out among those leaders who helped to change the conditions.

Clifford, in spite of his terribly hard life, starved and toiled to gain education. His intellect was recognised and he was given his chance in a Baptist college. All the degrees that the London University could offer him he earned. He graduated B.A., B.Sc., M.A., and LL.B. The opportunities Oxford and Cambridge could have given him were, of course, denied him, religious tests being still a shameful disability to Nonconformists desiring to enter either university. These also were one of the things this crusader helped to change.

Clifford had worked for a pittance in a pitiless industry, amid shameful conditions, and for intolerable hours. He never forgot this, and in later life he fought bravely for justice and honour and liberty to be accorded all men. The very memory of his early days and his terrible hardships made him the passionate antagonist of all tyrants and bigots. He was, however, never one to fight for himself, or for any selfish purpose. He was a born fighter, but a good loser also. He was as transparent as daylight, honest, chivalrous, a lover of freedom above all else. " No one has ever attempted to put a padlock on my lips : not that it would have done for them to try ! " he once said. Education, industry, temperance, the emancipation of women, peace—these were the great causes in which he crusaded. When he was fired by his burning indignation he was a formidable opponent; his enemies often called him an agitator, but he was never as little as that. He knew Christianity was meant to cover the whole of life, and he claimed it all for Jesus Christ. He thought of a Christian, not as a curator, but as a crusader. Through his own crusades he won national influence and honour. Many universities honoured him with degrees. Dr. Clifford believed in, and his life was an illustration of, the truth Lord Palmerston declared when he said : " In the long run English politics will follow the consciences of the Dissenters."*

The church at Praed Street, Marylebone, was one of the prominent Baptist centres in London. Its position in the West End made it accessible to large numbers of shop assistants who "lived in." But the church had been declining, and there was some question whether it was possible to revive it. The church members were, however, captivated by the young student from the Midland Baptist College. Clifford accepted the pastorate, determining, however, that he would go on with his studies. Clifford was young, twenty-two years of age, but at the same time very much matured by his

* Quoted in *Nonconformity*, by W. B. Selbie, M.A., D.D., p. 231.

experiences. He went on with his studies after settling in the church, taking his degrees with great brilliance, as has already been noted. He gathered young men and women into classes for all sorts of studies at the church. The building at Praed Street soon became too small for the crowds of young people who thronged it, and a new building was erected at Westbourne Park. This new church was destined to become one of the most famous in the country. It was Clifford's only church, and he was associated with it for sixty-five years.

The Baptist denomination owed much to John Clifford. For many years he was a trusted counsellor, and a keen worker upon many committees. He took great pains over details, and was never wearied by tedious committee routine. His help was sought in all the great causes of the denomination, and it was not sought in vain. In at least one sermon preached before the Assembly he made a deep impression. He closed one such sermon with these words : " If an old man may speak to his brethren, it shall be the word my mother gave me when I went to college: 'John, find out the teaching of Jesus, make yourself sure of that, and then stick to it, no matter what may come.'" He flung himself into the Brotherhood Movement with great enthusiasm. His white face, drawn features, massive brow, like some Old Testament prophet, had an irresistible appeal.

Clifford was one of those rare scholars who are also great orators; vast throngs loved him and hung on every word. He fought many battles; he was a crusader who was stirred to action by all distress or injustice. He was a teacher whose pupils found him an ardent but kindly teacher. He was also a pastor, with a great evangelistic fervour. His prayers climbed the heights; his sermons searched the soul; he was the real shepherd of his flock. He was always conscious of a Divine call, and he never lost his sense of fellowship with Christ. At the service in which he completed sixty years of ministry he said: "I believe that life is a whole, therefore I preach politics, civics, art, science, literature, as all affected by and included in religion. During all these years I have been preaching the Gospel of reconciliation." Those words describe the man and his message wonderfully well. He sought to claim the whole of life for his Saviour; he sought to proclaim the Gospel of reconciliation to all; and he feared no one so long as he obeyed his conscience. All who knew him were impressed by his courage and his fearlessness and his youthfulness in old age. At the time of his death at the age of eighty-seven he was writing a book which was to have as its title *The Zest of Life*!

John Clifford, with Spurgeon, did much to break down the awful dignity and aloofness of the Church and the minister of the time. Pompousness was the outstanding characteristic of the churches in the day when those two young ministers began their work in London. Both broke it by their emphasis upon personal evangelism, though in very different ways. Spurgeon opened his College, and Clifford opened a Westbourne Park Institute which grew into what was almost a working man's university. Both men were leading the Church out into new ventures; both were seeking the outsider.

John Clifford died as he would have wished. He went to a meeting of the Baptist Union Council on the morning of November 20, 1923. He was eighty-seven years of age but with unimpaired intellect he addressed the meeting, moving a resolution of sympathy with Dr. J. H. Shakespeare in his illness; then he made an appeal for personal evangelism. He sat down, his head drooped, his frail body slipped to the floor. The Council Chamber was cleared, but John Clifford was with his Master. That last speech was typical of Clifford : a benediction upon an old friend who was ill, and a challenge to a new generation not to forget the faith committed to it. He might have echoed the words he had spoken to youth on the evening of the first Armistice Sunday : " For the new world that is coming new men and women will be needed. As one who has been a Christian now for nearly seventy years I appeal to you to respond to the call of

Jesus. I have had my times of doubt and difficulty, and I have had my share of trouble; but ever Jesus has been my Companion and my Helper."

The memory of John Clifford, a great Englishman, a great world-citizen, a great Christian, will remain as a jewel in the heritage of coming generations. His passion for liberty has never been surpassed, but much that he fought for is again assailed, and today his spirit is needed—the spirit not simply of a politician, of a crusader for democracy and liberty, but the spirit of a Clifford who is these things because he has been captured by Christ, and brings his religion to bear on the whole of life, and claims it all for his God and his Christ. Such a spirit will "conquer modern democracy for Christ not less effectually than when it brought Roman imperialism to His feet in the early centuries."*

* *Baptist Principles,* by H. Wheeler Robinson, p. 74 (p. 79, reprint).

APPENDIX

For the purpose of this presentation of the story
of the Baptists, no mention has been made of the
two groups that existed for so many years.

The theology of the first Baptist Church was
Arminian—that is it believed in a general as distinct
from a particular Atonement. It believed that " the
work of Christ sufficed to redeem all men, and the
invitation of Christ was genuinely for all." The
earliest Baptist Confession of Faith was issued by
Thomas Helwys in 1611, and the fifth point states
clearly that " God would have all men saved and
come to the knowledge of the truth." These were
called General Baptists.

But a Particular Baptist, Calvinist, Church arose
about 1633 as an offshoot from the Congregational
Church. These people broke away from Congre-
gationalism because they became convinced that
baptism was not to be administered to infants but
to believers only. These people were Calvinists,
holding that the work of Christ was for particular
people only—the elect. At an Assembly in 1689,
attended by such men as Hanserd Knollys, William
Kiffin, and Benjamin Keach, a Confession of Faith
was agreed upon which laid down in Chapter III
that " by the decree of God . . . some men and angels
are predestinated or fore-ordained to eternal life

through Jesus Christ . . . the number cannot be either increased or diminished." The churches of this group grew and were organised in a similar manner to the General Baptists.

In 1770 the "New Connexion" was formed among General Baptists, bringing them nearer to the other body. The Calvinism of the Particular Baptists was also slowly modified, and in the 19th century most of the distinctions between them ceased to exist.

In these pages the life of the Baptist Church has been treated as a whole, and the distinctions ignored. But it is necessary, if the reader is intending to go on to the interesting study of one of the more detailed histories, to point out that such distinctions did exist.

BIBLIOGRAPHY

A History of the English Baptists. A. C. Underwood, M.A., B.Litt., D.D.

A History of British Baptists. W. T. Whitley, M.A., LL.D.

The Life and Faith of the Baptists. H. Wheeler Robinson, M.A., D.D.

Baptist Principles. H. Wheeler Robinson, M.A., D.D.

What Baptists Stand For. Henry Cook, M.A.

The Gathered Community. R. C. Walton, M.A.

The Fellowship of Believers. E. A. Payne, M.A., B.D., B.Litt.

The Church Awakes. E. A. Payne, M.A., B.D., B.Litt.

The Great Succession. E. A. Payne, M.A., B.D., B.Litt.

William Carey. S. Pearce Carey, M.A.

Andrew Fuller. G. Laws, D.D.

Timothy Richard. E. W. Price Evans, M.A.

Freedom in Jamaica. E. A. Payne, M.A., B.D., B.Litt.

John Clifford. G. W. Byrt.

C. H. Spurgeon. J. C. Carlile, C.H., C.B.E., D.D., D.Litt.

All the above are publications of The Carey Kingsgate Press, Ltd.